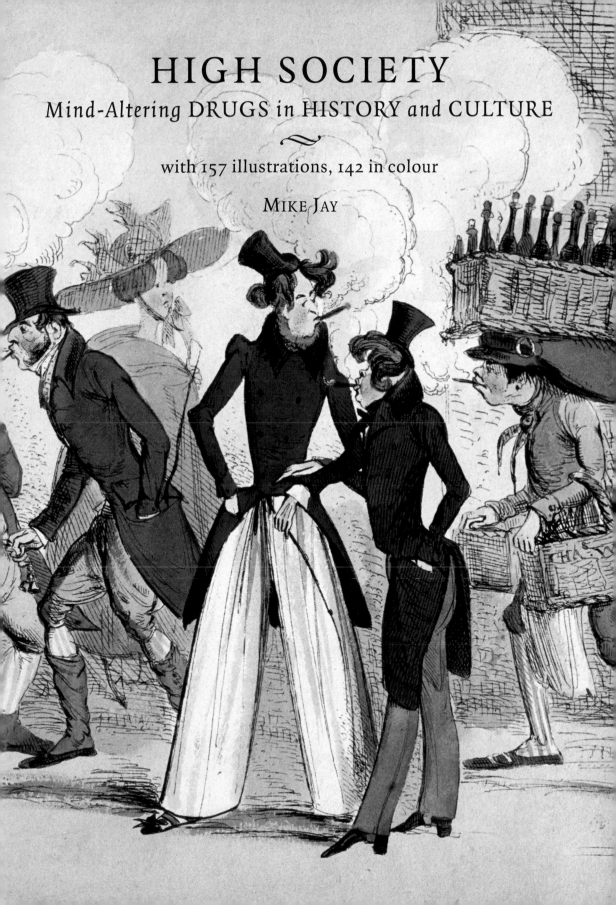

HIGH SOCIETY

Mind-Altering DRUGS in HISTORY and CULTURE

with 157 illustrations, 142 in colour

MIKE JAY

p. 1 *Marihuana: Weed with Roots in Hell*, detail from a 1930s anti-drug 'exploitation' movie poster.

pp. 2–3 *People Causing a Nuisance by Smoking in the Street*, coloured etching by H. Heath, London, 1827 (detail).

Right: A drawing by Paulino Barasana, an indigenous inhabitant of the Vaupés district of the Colombian Amazon, depicting his ayahuasca visions.

First published in the United Kingdom in 2010 by Thames & Hudson Ltd, 181A High Holborn, London WC1V 7QX

British Library Cataloguing-in-Publication Data

A catalogue record for this book is available from the British Library

ISBN 978-0-500-25172-0

Printed and bound in China

The Author and the Publisher would like to thank The Wellcome Trust for its help in making this publication possible. *High Society* was first published on the occasion of the exhibition of the same name, held at Wellcome Collection, London, 11 November 2010–27 February 2011.

wellcome collection

To find out about all our publications, please visit **www.thamesandhudson.com**. There you can subscribe to our e-newsletter, browse or download our current catalogue, and buy any titles that are in print.

CONTENTS

Foreword   6

A Universal Impulse 8

High Societies - The Evolution of Drugs - Animal
Intoxication - Drugs and Shamanism - Drugs and
Culture - The Culture of Kava - The Culture of Betel -
Drug Prohibitions - Drug Subcultures - The Cultures
of Ecstasy

From Apothecary to Laboratory   48

What Is a Drug? - Drugs in Antiquity - Renaissance
Herbals - Witches and Flying Ointments - The Invention
of Laudanum - Linnaeus and the Enlightenment -
The First Synthetic Drugs - Opium and the Romantics -
The Club des Haschischins - Freud and Cocaine -
Addiction and Drug Control - Mescaline, LSD and Beyond -
Drugs of the Future

The Drugs Trade   108

Drugs of the New World - The Psychoactive Revolution -
Tobacco in China, Tea in Europe - The Opium Wars -
The Anti-Opium campaign - Temperance and Prohibition -
The 'War on Drugs' - Epilogue: The Decline of Tobacco

Notes and Further Reading   174
Acknowledgments   186
Picture Credits   187
Index   188

Foreword

The fundamental urge to alter our consciousness in significant but controllable ways is, it seems, part of our hard-wiring. Very few people live their lives without using some kind of mind-altering substance, be it a cup of coffee, a glass of wine, sleeping pills, cigarettes or betel. The abundance of intoxicants and the myriad ways in which they are woven into the fabric of cultures around the world have left an extremely rich visual and material record, which this book explores. Moreover, drugs have significantly influenced social and cultural movements, defining entire subcultures from coffeehouses and opium dens to modern-day raves. Mind-altering substances answer the deep desire – need, even – we have to enhance and extend our ordinary experience of life.

As a habit, taking drugs seems directly related to our core interest in experimentation: the indulgence of our inclination to wonder 'What if?'. Accordingly, scientific enquiry into this aspect of human experience has progressively deepened and broadened in modern times. Since the eighteenth century, the development of new drugs has played out against a backdrop of pharmacological investigation and application, with traditional substances derived from plants and herbs augmented and then supplanted by synthetic chemicals. Though inevitably more subjective, the actual experience of drug consumption has also become an increasing focus of enquiry, frequently through self-experiment. Here the approach of science has gone hand in hand with the practices of art to explore the

A waiter pours a drink for a customer in a painting of an eighteenth-century London coffee house (detail) (*above*); ceremonial drinking of kava in the Friendly Islands (Tonga), engraving by W. Sharp after John Webber (detail) (*below right*); illustration of a cannabis plant from *De historia stirpium commentarii insignes* by the Bavarian physician Leonhart Fuchs (1542) (*opposite*); a Mandarin sits on a mat, smoking a long opium pipe, in a coloured aquatint by Swiss artist Sigismond Himely, c. 1820 (*opposite above*).

impact of drugs on creativity. More recently, in a century when the social impact of drug consumption has emerged as an ever-more-threatening 'social menace', science has also been called upon for guidance in tackling the problem of addiction.

High Society is an intriguingly multi-layered account of humanity's long and elaborate dance with mind-altering drugs. It was written as an extension of Mike Jay's advisory and curatorial work on an exhibition of the same name presented at Wellcome Collection, London. Wellcome Collection was not conceived as a conventional venue for the dissemination and popularization of scientific knowledge. Instead its approach has been to think in public – 'out loud', as it were – about medical science and its connections with art and the rest of life. The subject of drugs, with its rich history of scientific experimentation, literary and artistic inspiration, economic opportunity, societally encoded behaviour and fundamental biological effects, is an ideal focus for an institution dedicated to investigating science as a vibrant part of culture.

Ken Arnold
Head of Public Programmes, Wellcome Collection, London

A Universal Impulse

Every society on earth is a high society. As the sun rises in the east, caffeine is infused and sipped across China in countless forms of dried, smoked and fermented tea. From the archipelagos of Indonesia and New Guinea through Thailand, Burma and India, a hundred million chewers of betel prepare their quids of areca nut, pepper leaf and caustic lime ash, press it between their teeth and expectorate the day's first mouthful of crimson saliva. Across the cities of Thailand, Korea and China, potent and illicit preparations such as *ya'aba*, home-cooked amphetamine pills swallowed or smoked, propel a young generation through the double working shifts of economic boomtime, or burn up the empty hours of unemployment, before igniting the clubs and bars of the urban nightscape.

As the sun tracks across towards the afternoon, the rooftop terraces of Yemen's medieval mud-brick cities fill with men gathering to converse and chew khat through the scorching heat of the day. Across the concrete jungles of the Middle East, millions without the means for a midday meal make do with a heap of sugar stirred into a small cup of strong black tea. As the working day in Europe draws to a close, the traffic through the bars of the city squares begins to pick up, and high-denomination euro notes are surreptitiously exchanged for wraps of cocaine and ecstasy. In the cities of West Africa, the highlife clubs are thick with cannabis smoke, while in the forests initiates of the Bwiti religion sweat their way through their three-day intoxication by the hallucinogenic root *iboga*, during which they see the visions that will guide them through the passage to adulthood.

When daylight reaches the western hemisphere, it illuminates the broadest spectrum of drug cultures on the planet. Across North America's cities, the sidewalks throng with office workers clutching lattes and espressos, while giant trucks thunder down interstate highways delivering tobacco and alcohol on a scale now rivalled by the industrial marijuana plantations concealed in giant polytunnels and warehouses among the forest tracts of California and Canada. Further south, the Huichol people of Mexico, despite the mesh fences and enclosures spreading across their ancient hunting grounds, still make their desert pilgrimage to harvest peyote cactus for their rituals, while street

Opposite: A young man smokes *ganja* (cannabis) in the slums of Dhaka in Bangladesh, where it has been used for centuries and was made illegal only in 1984. The World Health Organization estimates that cannabis is used by around 150 million people across the globe.

children in the *barrios* of Colombia and Brazil stupefy themselves with petrol-soaked cocaine residue and aerosol sprays. And in the Amazon, dozens of tribes, as they have since time immemorial, squat around fires powdering, toasting and brewing the seeds, roots and leaves of the world's most diverse mind-altering flora.

Finally the sun sets across the islands of the south Pacific, the most remote outposts of humanity. Here, almost all the drugs consumed by the rest of the world remain unknown: even alcohol and tobacco are costly imports, rare outside the urban centres. But from the middle of the afternoon, the men have been drifting in from their gardens and plantations to grate, chew and soak kava root for their evening brew. As the sun sets, they congregate in huts to drink it from coconut shells and share some whispered conversation, or squat alone on the beach to listen to its voice in the surf, as the sunset fades to darkness.

Drug cultures are endlessly varied, but drugs in general are more or less ubiquitous among our species. The celebrated list of 'human universals' compiled by the anthropologist Donald E. Brown includes 'mood- or consciousness-altering techniques and/or substances' as one of the essential components of human culture, along with music, conflict resolution, language and play. But there is little consensus regarding the origins of this universal impulse, which essential human traits it serves and how far back into our past its roots extend. Some have posited a primordial moment of discovery when proto-humans first encountered plants that expanded their minds to generate new forms of thought and language. Others have argued that such a moment may be encoded in our shared origin myths, perhaps in stories of a fruit that bestowed the knowledge of good and evil. Nevertheless, it seems that the discovery of intoxicants is a drama in which even the remote human past is a very recent episode. The plants that contain these substances evolved alongside our animal antecedents, and many developed such chemicals because of their physiological effects on creatures like ourselves. We were taking drugs long before we were human.

Drugs, and our response to them, are the product of an elaborate evolutionary dance between the plant and animal kingdoms that has been underway for at least 300 million years. Coniferous trees began producing tannins to deter fungal parasites, and bitter saponines to repel wood-boring insects. Flowering plants, when they emerged during the Cretaceous period, developed more complex nitrogen-based alkaloids in their fruit and leaves. These compounds, typically bitter to the taste, are toxic to some animals but produce pleasant effects in others. The

Khat chewers in Sana'a, the capital of Yemen. The cultivation, transport, trade and consumption of the fresh khat leaf is the mainstay of local economies across many parts of East Africa and the Arabian peninsula.

capsaicin in chilli peppers, for example, is both a deterrent and a stimulant, killing parasites but encouraging the release of endorphins in mammals (while birds, on which the chilli depends for its dispersal, lack the chemical receptor that causes it to function as an irritant). Plant families often generate a spectrum of related alkaloids with both mental and physical effects: the nightshades, for example, manufacture the poisons in raw potatoes, the bug-killing and brain-rewarding nicotine in tobacco, and the hallucinogenic deliriants in daturas and belladonna.

Long before humans first appeared, this profuse natural pharmacopeia encouraged an equally wide variety of drug-seeking behaviours. Many animals root out and consume plant drugs for medical purposes – to poison intestinal parasites, for example – but there are also abundant examples of the deliberate pursuit of intoxication. Cats abandon themselves to the ecstasy of catnip, which has little effect on humans but causes felines to head-twitch, salivate, give love-bites and apparently experience sexual hallucinations: in the wild, the plant may perform the function of bringing females into heat. Siberian bears and reindeer seek

Teniers in et excud cum privilegio.

out fly agaric mushrooms and appear to relish their mind-altering effects. Migrating birds make regular seasonal detours to gorge on fermented fruits. For many villages across the Indian subcontinent, a herd of drunken elephants on the rampage after feasting on rotten windfalls or raiding illegal stills is an all too familiar hazard. Our closest relatives, the primates, display many sophisticated drug-seeking behaviours. Baboons chew tobacco in the wild, and apes in captivity readily learn the habit of smoking it. Male mandrills in Gabon have even been observed to dig up and eat the hallucinogenic *iboga* root, then wait for an hour for its effects to take hold before engaging rivals in combat.

In many human cultures, the origin stories of plant-derived drugs involve tales of people observing and copying the habits of animals. In Ethiopia, for example, the discovery of coffee is attributed to goatherders who observed their flock becoming frisky and high-spirited after consuming coffee beans. Goats are very fond of coffee, and modern plantations must be robustly fenced against them; their taste for the effects of caffeine may have prompted the plant, which spreads its seeds via animal droppings, to produce it. Theirs is a long-standing symbiosis, though human participation in the cycle is relatively new. The practice of coffee drinking seems only to have developed around the tenth century AD –

recently enough, perhaps, for the legends of its discovery to have some historical validity. It seems plausible that the practice of roasting the seeds of one among many hard, bitter and inedible desert shrubs and then percolating boiling water through them might have emerged only in modern times, and with some peculiar prompting.

Plants, then, use their drugs to nudge and manipulate the animal kingdom, repelling some species and attracting others; but what benefits do animals derive from drugs? It is often assumed that they consume them instinctively for chemical rewards: the stimulation of neurochemicals such as dopamine and serotonin, and the pleasurable sensations they deliver to the brain. Indeed, the modern neurological understanding of drugs leans heavily on the responses of laboratory animals: the 'addictiveness' of substances such as cocaine and opiates is measured by, for example, how many times a caged rat will press a lever to receive a dose. But there is more to animal drug-taking than reflex response. Environment is also a factor: many animals, for example, are more inclined to take drugs in captivity. This tendency was explored in a startling series of experiments by the Canadian addiction psychologist Bruce Alexander.

Alexander's clinical work involved tests on laboratory rats. Initially the rats were kept individually in small cages with two drinking bottles,

Below: The Rat Park experiments conducted by Bruce Alexander in the late 1970s at Simon Fraser University in British Columbia, Canada. Some of the laboratory rats typically housed in cramped and solitary cages (*left*) were moved to a spacious, open-plan social environment (*right*), where their drug use diminished dramatically.

one containing plain water and the other morphine solution, which were weighed daily to generate behavioural data. But Alexander became curious about the effects of environment, and constructed alongside the cages a habitat that became known as Rat Park. Several rats, who are naturally gregarious, were housed together in a large vivarium enriched with wheels, balls and other playthings, on a deep bed of aromatic cedar shavings and with plenty of space for breeding and private interactions. Pleasant woodland vistas were even painted on the surrounding walls.

In Rat Park, he discovered, drug use diminished markedly: some rats reduced their morphine intake to one-twentieth that of their caged neighbours. Even if pre-addicted to morphine, they would suffer withdrawals rather than maintain their habit. When the morphine water was sweetened with sugar, most of the rats still chose plain water, though they would drink the sugared water if Alexander also added naloxone, which blocks morphine's effects. It seemed that the standard experiments were measuring not the addictiveness of opiates but the stresses inflicted on lab rats caged in solitary confinement, with catheters inserted into their jugular veins.

Such experiments do not disprove the claim that animals take drugs for their chemical rewards, but they do indicate that the impulse to take drugs is more than a simple behavioural reflex. In humans, of course, the variables become far more complicated. Sensory pleasure is an obvious component of most drug use, though the definitions of pleasure are as varied as human culture itself. But some drugs offer strictly functional benefits. The ability to alter consciousness in dramatic but controllable ways has many uses, and there is much evidence to suggest that humans have long used such drugs instrumentally: even, in some cases, elaborating their entire social systems around the heightened states of consciousness such substances produce.

Perhaps the earliest drug artefacts in the archaeological record are two chillum-style pipes fashioned from hollowed-out puma bones, excavated in 1973 from a cave high in the Andes of north-west Argentina and radiocarbon-dated to before 2000 BC. The pipes were found to contain the burnt residue of the seeds of the mountain shrub *Anadenanthera*, a rich source of dimethyltryptamine. DMT, as it is known, is among the most powerful naturally occurring hallucinogens. When smoked or snuffed in sufficient quantities, it produces a rapid reaction of extreme nausea and often convulsive vomiting, accompanied by a few minutes of exquisitely strange, beautiful or terrifying visions.

A carved stone head from the ancient temple site of Chavín de Huantar in the Peruvian Andes, with grimacing jaws and mucus flowing from its nostrils. The heads form a sequence representing the transformation from human to jaguar under the influence of DMT-containing snuff.

With the appearance of monumental architecture in South America, the use of such drugs is attested in more detail. The ceremonial centre of Chavín, constructed in the Peruvian Andes in the centuries around 1000 BC, is surrounded by towering stone walls studded with a series of grotesque stone heads frozen in various stages of transformation from human to jaguar. As the heads grin and grimace, eyes bulging and fangs sprouting, streams of mucus pour from their noses: a telltale sign of the snuffing of powdered *Anadenanthera* seeds, which is further attested by the distinctive snuff trays excavated from similar sites across Peru, Bolivia and Chile. The drug's effects were, it seems, understood as a process of shapeshifting between human and monstrous feline forms.

The notion that DMT-containing powders and potions transform their human subjects into animals – particularly predators, such as big cats or snakes – remains widespread throughout the many shamanic cultures of the Amazon region today. Animal transformation is not regarded as pleasurable: indeed, in both ancient and modern traditions it

is represented as physically unpleasant and emotionally traumatic. Just as
the stone heads on Chavín's walls appear in a transport of agony rather
than ecstasy, the Amazon cultures who still use DMT-containing snuffs,
or infusions such as ayahuasca, typically describe the ordeal as terrifying.
The drug is taken not for sensory gratification, but for immersion in a
collective mental and spiritual world in which the participants become
something more than human.

Between 1966 and 1969, the Austrian-born anthropologist Gerardo
Reichel-Dolmatoff made a series of field trips to study the use of hallucinogenic snuffs among the Tukano Indian groups in the Vaupés area
of the Colombian Amazon. These groups have little in the way of social
hierarchies, chiefs or councils of elders; conflicts are largely mediated
by shamans, a category of adult males with specialist knowledge of
plants, hunting or healing. The shamans' activities are almost always
conducted under the influence of a snuff prepared from the DMT-rich sap
sweated out of the bark of various trees of the *Virola* genus. Powdered and
propelled into the sinuses through a hollow stone or bone tube, the sap
produces a state of heightened awareness in which diseases are treated

Opposite and above: Some Tukano groups consume DMT in the form of ayahuasca, a bitter tea that contains the drug in combination with other mind-altering plants. These two figures (opposite) are forest spirits seen in ayauhasca visions: a husband and wife holding batons covered in sickness that they spread among humans. The decorative art that covers Tukano clothes, ornaments, pottery and houses (above) is almost entirely drawn from ayauhasca visions.

and weather and game patterns predicted. But when large doses of snuff are taken, it is universally recognized among the Tukano that the shamans will turn into jaguars.

When Reichel-Dolmatoff attempted to establish precisely what this transformation entailed, he received a bewildering variety of explanations. The 'jaguar complex', as he termed it, operated across many levels of meaning. On one level, it described the physical sensations produced by the drug: snuffing produces a painful burning sensation followed by convulsive nausea, and shamans in the grip of these symptoms are said to be jaguars writhing and 'turning their bellies up'. They were also consciously imitating jaguars: many shamans had personal collections of jaguar skin, claws and teeth. But they were also genuinely believed to be shifting form, taking on powers that make them capable of bloody acts of predation and revenge. It follows from this that a jaguar encountered in the wild may not truly be a jaguar, but rather a shaman in feline 'dress'. Shamans acting in this way are able to enter the dreams of others in jaguar form. As they wander in the forest, their jaguar 'dress' can also guide them to the trails of 'real' jaguars, which they might witness, as some zoologists have, chewing on hallucinogenic vines and 'turning their bellies up' as the effects take hold.

On the surface, the transformation of shaman into jaguar seemed to be accepted as real by all Reichel-Dolmatoff's subjects. Young men regaled him with bloodthirsty tales of rapes and murders that they had undertaken in feline form, often of friends or close kin; claw-marks and bloodstained whiskers were offered up as physical proof. But these terrifying tales tended to evaporate under scrutiny. The alleged victims were still alive and unharmed: the acts of violence seemed to have taken place in a parallel world. Indeed, Reichel-Dolmatoff's informants acknowledged that 'real' jaguars are not particularly ferocious or dangerous, and are far more likely to flee from humans than to attack them. The shaman's transformation into a jaguar was a symbolic theatre in which impulses of aggression and revenge could be acted out physically and tangibly, but without real-life consequences.

Yet the jaguar transformation was more than charade or a drug-induced fantasy. Under the influence of the snuff, shamans found themselves awakening into a state of hyper-consciousness in which they could see, hear, smell and understand aspects of reality normally hidden from view. The idea that they had transformed into jaguars made sense of these sensations: they were in possession of the uncanny night vision of the predator, its speed and agility, its preternaturally acute hearing. They were able to observe the world through new eyes, to receive unfamiliar impressions, and to expand the store of natural knowledge demanded by their role: the positions of the stars, the habits of other animals, the patterns of plant growth, the fluctuations of weather and climate, the hidden weave of nature itself. Used in this way, drugs can operate as a kind of sensory prosthetic: just as a diving suit allows humans temporary access to a normally hostile and alien world, *Virola* snuff allows the shaman to encompass a world populated by many different forms of consciousness and to glimpse a perspective beyond the limits of the human.

Drugs can bestow remarkable powers, but only to those who are primed to receive them. The hallucinatory derangement of *Virola* snuff will overwhelm anyone who ingests enough of it, but for most it will be recalled (if at all) as a fever dream of fragmentary impressions, dominated by sensations of burning sinuses and overwhelming nausea. It is an intensely personal ordeal, but can only be understood within a social context. Unlike animal intoxication, human drug use is part of a web of verbal and symbolic culture, and it is here that its shared meanings reside.

In 1953 Howard S. Becker, a young sociologist and jazz enthusiast, published a now-classic paper entitled 'Becoming a Marihuana User'. His musical interests had led him to study the lifestyles of New York's jazz

Opposite: The jazz scene in postwar New York, in which Howard Becker conducted his research, was an epicentre of the cannabis culture that became a global phenomenon in the 1960s. One of the earliest accounts was the 1946 memoir of the Jewish saxophonist Milton 'Mezz' Mezzrow, who explained: 'tea puts a musician in a real masterly sphere, and that's why so many jazzmen have used it'.

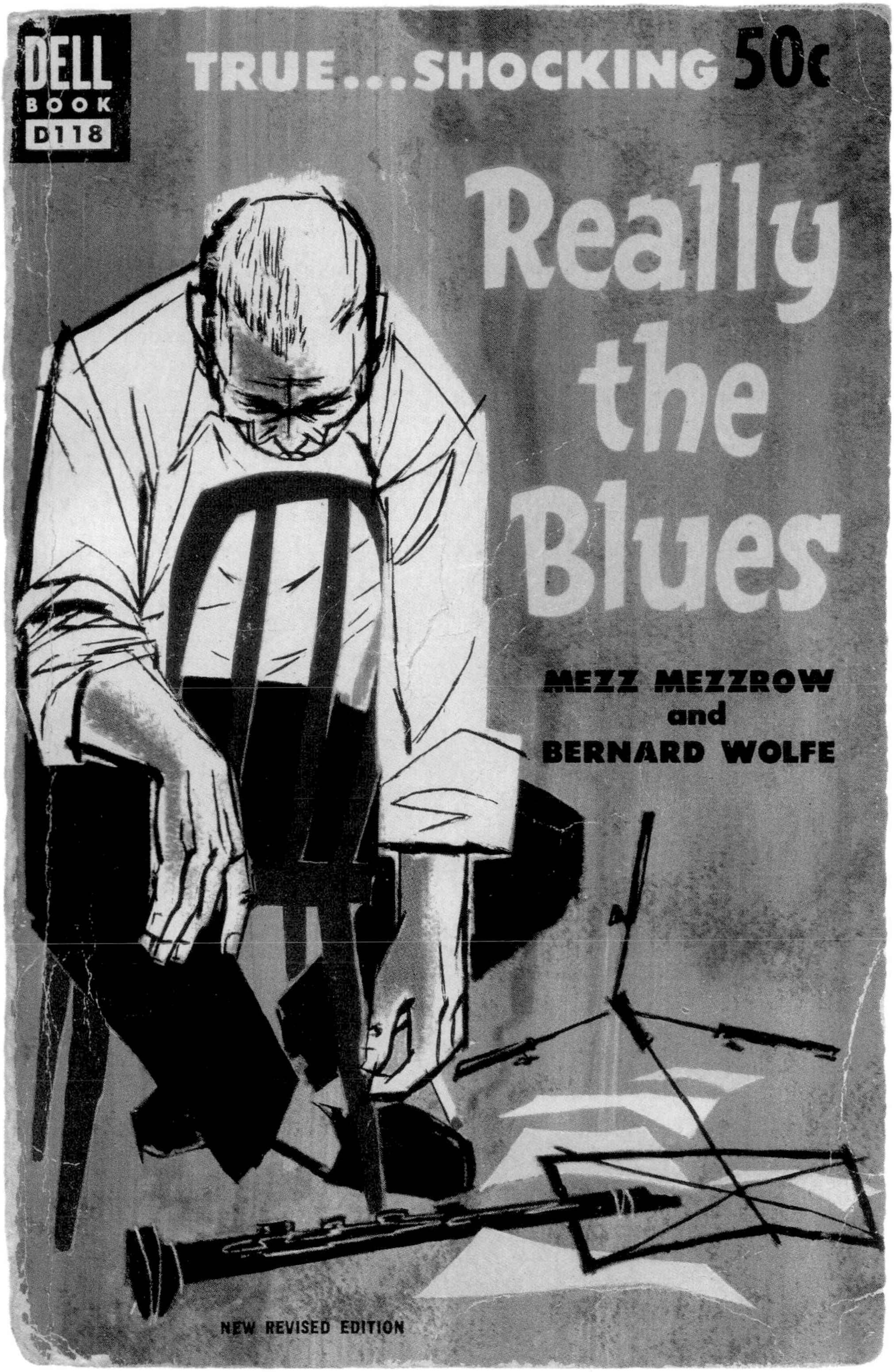

DELL
BOOK
D118

TRUE...SHOCKING 50¢

Really the Blues

MEZZ MEZZROW
and
BERNARD WOLFE

NEW REVISED EDITION

subculture, and he had focused on the practice of smoking cannabis, a habit widespread within his study group but regarded as deviant in the cultural mainstream. He began an informal project of interviewing users to understand how this practice was learned and transmitted.

What Becker discovered was a three-stage model that has since been applied to drug cultures across the world. The first stage, 'Learning the Technique', involved the technical challenge of ingesting a sufficient dose of the drug – in this case, learning to inhale correctly, and to hold the smoke in the lungs for a sufficient length of time. But this was not enough to get high in and of itself: most first-time users felt no effects at all. A second stage, 'Learning to Perceive the Effects', was essential. This required the user to believe that there were indeed effects to be perceived, and to cultivate a gradual physical recognition of them: head-spinning, rubbery legs or hunger pangs. But even when perceived, it was not obvious to the user that these effects were desirable. The third stage, 'Learning to Enjoy the Effects', could only be grasped within a culture where the drug's effects were valued: light-headedness was a cue for gig-gling and verbal flights of fancy, hunger pangs led to enjoyable snacking binges, feelings of anxiety or paranoia were acknowledged and soothed with camaraderie and humour.

Becker's observations challenged the consensus view of 1950s American psychiatry that marijuana users represented a deviant and crim-inal minority whose aberrant appetites led them to drug use. It was, he argued, the opposite: they had joined a subculture within which drugs became pleasurable. 'Marihuana use', he concluded, 'is a function of the individual's conception of marihuana and of the uses to which it can be put'. People in straight society shunned marijuana not because they were virtuous, but because there was no reward to be gained from it: even if they felt the effects, they would lack the context in which to enjoy them.

The physical effects of most drugs are initially unpleasant, and would be perceived as toxic unless they were culturally valued, shared and sanctioned. The first glass of beer is unpleasantly sour; the first sip of red wine burns the mouth; the first lungful of tobacco produces coughing, low blood pressure and nausea. Modern drug cultures, by validating the exploration of unfamiliar tastes and mental states, have converted many substances from poison to exotic pleasure. 'Magic' mushrooms, for example, are now consumed with the expectation of a colourful and mind-expanding trip, but historical accounts of accidental ingestions show that, without such expectations, their effects were typically taken to be the painful and alarming onset of poisoning. The drug habits of one culture often disgust another, at least until the new drug is socialized and normalized: drugs may be universal, but they are also an acquired taste.

Throughout history, the spread of foreign drugs has been socially divisive, eagerly adopted by some and fiercely resisted by others.

But drugs are not always divisive. They can also reinforce cultural values, strengthening and formalizing them, often to the point where vital exchanges become inconceivable without them. The role of kava in many cultures across the South Pacific offers a striking example.

Kava is a narcotic drink produced by grinding and soaking the root tubers of *Piper methysticum*, a large plant of the pepper family. Since it must be drunk fresh, preparing kava is a process that consumes a significant proportion of every day. Roots must be rubbed clean with coconut husks, stripped, peeled and shredded – these days usually with an old cheese grater into a plastic bowl, but in the most traditional villages by chewing the root and spitting the macerated pulp into a banana leaf. Although this process

Below: In the Pacific nation of Fiji, kava is drunk to welcome guests in both private and public ceremonies. Here Queen Elizabeth II is offered kava in the traditional receptacle, a coconut shell, on her state visit in 1982.

appears unhygenic, kava-drinkers rarely catch diseases from one another: in addition to its mind-altering qualities, the root is also antibacterial and antifungal. The syphilis that spread across the region with Western contact affected kava-drinkers markedly less than their neighbours.

Once prepared, the drink is poured into coconut shells, which are knocked back quickly and cleanly: although kava has an exalted cultural status, it is still not reckoned to taste very nice. It is a muddy pale-brown suspension with a peppery burn and a distinctive numbing effect on the lips and throat. Other effects soon follow: a fullness in the head, a rush of warm feelings and a clumsy, stumbling gait. Sounds become louder and light harsher: it is good manners to whisper among fellow-drinkers and to dim paraffin lamps. After a few hours of gentle trance, it promotes a sound night's sleep, making it a better complement to working routines than alcohol. In equally marked contrast to alcohol, which has had destructive effects on many Pacific cultures, kava encourages positive social behaviours such as generosity and sensitivity, cordial conversation and comfortable silence.

For these reasons kava is an ancient and essential element, both symbolic and practical, in social interaction. Kava-drinking, like the Native American peace pipe, is a communion through which friendly relations are established, contracts sealed and hostilities set aside. Kava roots are exchanged as gifts between neighbours, and more formally between families at weddings and funerals. Whether drunk or exchanged, the presence of kava signals a hiatus in niggling rivalries and social tensions and an opportunity for a fresh start in individual or group relations. It can even smooth over major inter-group conflicts and civil wars: once the 'big men' or elders of rival groups have formally made peace in a kava ceremony, all resentments are truly dead and buried. Its time-honoured role is reflected in modern political protocol, particularly in Tonga and Fiji, where foreign presidents, royalty and even popes are publicly welcomed with kava ceremonies. Generally, governments across the Pacific are keen to encourage its use, which stimulates the local economy and mitigates the negative social consequences of alcohol.

The origins of kava use are the subject of many myth-cycles in the South Pacific. Most prominent among them is the story that humans discovered the wild root by watching rats eating it and staggering clumsily back for more. Botanically, the origins of the kava plant are enigmatic: it is a sterile clone from a long-forgotten source, a cultivar surviving only through human agency. For the cultures that use it, kava therefore also serves as a sacred conduit to their ancestral inheritance. Alongside its public and social role, this private aspect of kava is highly valued: it is at dusk, regarded in Melanesia as a time of especially strong ancestral

Opposite: Fresh kava being prepared by an indigenous group in Arnhem Land, Northern Australia. During the 1980s, missionaries and tribal leaders from Melanesia began to introduce kava to Australian communities ravaged by alcoholism, but it has now been banned by the federal government.

presence, that kava ceremonies are held. It is drunk in graveyards to allow
the living to listen to the voices of the departed: revelations received in
this way are not taken as the utterance of the one who heard them, but
as messages from a deeper source. In this sense, kava-drinking allows
individuals to act as disembodied oracles for the community at large.

Kava, then, can be seen as a universal solvent: a drug that has insinuated itself into almost every aspect of life. Public gatherings of all kinds
depend on its mediating influence; at the same time, it offers privileged
access to the deepest recesses of the private self. The diversity of its roles
overspills the borders, in other contexts rigorously defined, between
sacred and secular. On some islands, its use is confined to priestly cere-
monials; on others, the towns are full of late-night kava bars. There is
much evidence, even during the short period of recorded history since

Above and above right: A kava ceremony hosted by the royal family of Tonga, from a sketch made in 1777 by John Webber, the artist on Captain James Cook's third expedition to the Pacific (*above*). In contrast to subsequent colonists and missionaries who banned the practice, Cook hosted kava ceremonies in his private cabin on the HMS *Resolution*, and in Hawaii was presented with a fine ceremonial bowl (*above right*).

Captain James Cook's first contacts with the region, that such patterns of use are remarkably fluid: old taboos have been superseded and religious traditions modified in response to new developments such as colonial regimes or global trade. In Fiji, for example, kava circles have become more formal since Western contact, while in Vanuatu the traditional village setting of the *nakamal* has been supplemented by more casual drop-in urban kava bars. Often the sanction to change the rules comes from revelations received during the kava trance itself: the drug even provides its own mechanism to renew its charter with the society it serves.

Yet kava, while unifying societies in so many ways, also exemplifies the role that drugs can play in dividing and stratifying them. The most obvious in this case, and perhaps most typical overall, is the way its use divides the genders. In most Pacific cultures, kava use is an exclusively male preserve, and the marker of broader male domains in society. The *nakamal*, the meeting ground in the village where kava is prepared, is taboo to women. The long hours of kava preparation constitute a forum for exclusively male discussion and decision-making, as does participation in the kava trance. Similar gender distinctions are enforced in many traditional cultures across the globe, from ayahuasca-drinking in the Amazon to tobacco-smoking in Arabia. Though often rationalized with the view that intoxication is socially or biologically inappropriate for women, limiting drug-taking to men seems to play a more active role in reinforcing and formalizing a primary distinction between the sexes. It demarcates a female sphere of mundane domestic activity, centred around childcare, housekeeping and the preparation of food, by creating an alternative male sphere centred around ritual, ceremonial occasion and heightened consciousness.

There is no evidence that this strict demarcation has its roots in human biology. Rather, traditional prohibitions against women using intoxicants simply illustrate another way in which drugs insinuate themselves into cultures: by becoming a means of signalling boundaries. When such cultural prohibitions are not strictly enforced, drug use by women tends to become normalized: in the modern kava bars of the urban Pacific, women drink as freely as men, and the pleasure drugs of Western subcultures, particularly cocaine and ecstasy, are equally popular across the gender divide.

Immediately to the west of the kava cultures of the Pacific extends a vast territory, stretching from New Guinea, north to China and west to Madagascar, where the habit of betel-chewing dates back far into prehistory. The 'quid' that is chewed may contain many ingredients, but three are essential: the nut of the areca palm, wrapped in the leaf of the betel pepper, which is spread with a paste of lime ash. The lime precipitates and releases alkaloids in the two plants that combine to produce a mild and agreeable combination of alertness, relaxation and euphoria, as well as aiding digestion and stimulating the production of red-stained saliva.

Although the betel habit is rich in sacred symbolism, with countless mythological stories woven around the origins of its ingredients, it is essentially a secular practice whose domain is one of leisure, hospitality and luxury. Women partake as frequently as men – more so, in fact, in societies such as Indonesia where men increasingly smoke clove cigarettes in its place. Like tobacco, it generates a low-level social economy where peasant women squat in markets, village squares and street corners to exchange small packages of nut, leaf and lime for the spare

Opposite: A tribesman from Ifugao in the mountainous interior of Luzon, northern Philippines, chewing betel. Habitual chewing can cause chronic damage to teeth and gums but the red staining it produces is seen in many cultures as a mark of beauty.

Right: The betel quid has many variants but three essential components: the nut of the areca palm, spread with lime ash and folded in the leaf of the betel pepper. When chewed, the lime releases the alkaloids in the other two plants.

Below: Women conducting 'betelnut bisnis' in a market in the Solomon Islands beyond New Guinea, at the eastern extremity of betel culture.

Above: A seventeenth-century
Mughal prince reclining among
the traditional 'enjoyments of
life', including an ornate betel
set in the foreground.

coins of labourers and shopkeepers, for whom betel buys a few minutes
of private relaxation or convivial gossip. Its recreational virtues are sanctioned by centuries of tradition: a sixth-century Indian text lists it as one of
the eight enjoyments of life (along with incense, women, clothes, music,
beds, food and flowers).

As with any such commodity, there are products and prices to suit all
tastes. Some prefer their areca nuts young and soft, while others will pay
more for the astringent tannins that develop when they are dried and
cured. Sellers need to know their market: the betel that fetches the best
price in the highlands will often be regarded as inferior on the coast.
Beyond its essential ingredients, costly spices can be added – cloves,
musk, camphor – for sweet breath. Those who wish to display generous
hospitality will buy fresh betel, perhaps of a higher quality than their daily
chew. Elegant betel habits are a sign of refinement: young women will be
judged on how neatly they roll their leaf into a quid. The habit is one of
private gratification, but its outward signs communicate clear messages
of sophistication and character. As with coffee or wine, the rituals of
preparation and consumption socialize a desire for intoxication that
might otherwise appear unseemly or selfish.

The various components of the betel chew have, over the centuries,
lent themselves to a profusion of utensils through which different grada-
tions of wealth and taste are expressed and a decorative aesthetic is

Above and right: 'Betel nut
beauties' are a familiar part of
the urban landscape of Taiwan,
where their brightly lit glass
kiosks line the main traffic
routes. They sell ready-rolled
betel quids to motorists and
truck drivers, for whose
attention they compete with
their skimpy and alluring outfits.

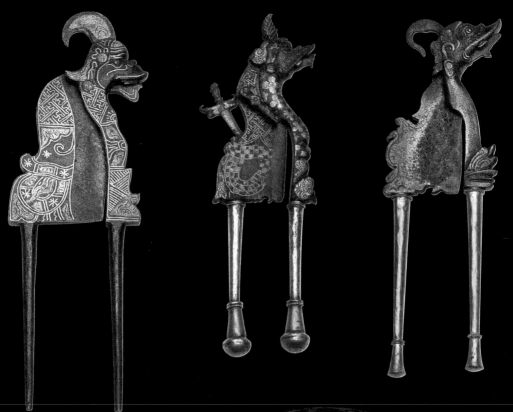

Above and right: Betel accessories are part of the ornamental tradition of most South Asian cultures. These Balinese betel cutters (*above*), used for slicing the areca nut, are modelled on familiar characters from the *wayang* shadow-puppet theatre. The lacquerware lid of a Burmese betel box (*right*) opens to reveal highly polished compartments that hold the ingredients for the quid.

explored and refined. The practice requires, at the bare minimum, a tray on which to lay out the ingredients; it is also desirable to have a cutter to slice the nut, a vase or pouch to contain the leaves, a pot to hold the lime and a spatula to spread it on the leaf. For most villagers these will be made of everyday materials such as wood or rattan, but for those aspiring to higher status they are the perfect pretext for a conspicuous display of wealth. The first European visitors to south-east Asia were staggered by the ornate betel sets used by the royalty of Khmer and Siam. Gold and silver boxes, cutters and bowls, enamelled, chased and filigreed, were accompanied by solid gold spittoons, and carried by a procession of 'betel slaves' constantly busy with lime, nut and leaf, pestles and mortars, lip salves and holders for quids awaiting consumption.

This type of royal display set the tone for courtiers, nobles and merchants, and established a diversity of regional styles and materials. Classic Burmese betel-ware consisted of round lacquered boxes, intricately worked with designs in red, black and gold, and opening to reveal a nest of smaller polished trays and implements. In the Malay peninsula, specialist metalworking trades turned to producing sets in pale brass alloys, filigreed with Arabic script; in Indonesia, cutters were worked into the sinuous shapes of *wayang* shadow-puppets. The economy of betel extends far beyond the drug itself. Even in its most costly forms, spiced and scented with musk and ambergris, it is only the springboard for a cult of material indulgence: formed around a shared and cherished intoxication, but elaborated into an endless variety of ways to express cultural identity.

From Amazonian tree-bark resins toasted on the embers of campfires to betel quids offered to kings on solid-gold salvers, drugs present themselves in almost every imaginable form. The intoxications they offer are equally diverse, from mild stimulation to life-threatening ordeal; and their social roles span a range from natural sacrament to luxury merchandise. But there is an alternative form of drug culture that has, over the last century, come to prominence across the modern world: one that defines itself not by its use of drugs, but by its prohibition of them.

In most cultures throughout history, only a small number of drugs were in common use. The remainder were not explicitly forbidden; there was no need, since they lacked the cultural framework to make them desirable. Official drug prohibitions are the exception rather than the rule, but they are not an exclusively modern phenomenon. The most familiar historical example, perhaps, is the prohibition of alcohol across much of the Islamic world.

Above: Alcohol intoxication was a conspicuous motif in the Roman culture of luxury. In this mural from the House of the Chaste Lovers in Pompeii, two prostitutes ply the victor of a drinking competition with more wine from a drinking-horn, while his defeated rival lies insensible beside him.

Like the drug prohibitions of the twentieth century, this proscription of alcohol was one manifestation among many of a dramatic social rupture. The culture that rose to power with Islam defined itself in opposition to the region's previous rulers, the city-dwelling merchants of the Mediterranean coast. The conquerors were nomadic traders who brought with them a desert culture that stressed the virtues of dignity and self-control, and expressed them through frugal and ascetic habits. They saw the urban merchants as a decadent and corrupt elite, whose vices were exemplified by the wine on which they squandered their wealth in boorish intoxication. With the ascendancy of Islam, the luxuries of the city were replaced by the austerity of the camel train, the villa by the desert tent, the stuffed divan by the simple cushion on the ground. The prohibition of alcohol evolved from individual acts of religious observance to edicts against public drunkenness, and finally to a universal taboo; in the process, it confirmed the new cultural hegemony.

As with all drug prohibitions, however, it was technically not a
prohibition but a substitution. The vacuum created by alcohol was filled,
over time, with a broad spectrum of stimulants and narcotics. A small,
strong cup of coffee or tea – astringent and parsimonious of resources –
took the role of wine as a marker of hospitality. Other stimulants, including
kola nut in the Sudan and khat across east Africa and western Arabia,
became integral to social exchange and leisure. Coffee emerged to
rival tea; tobacco became (and remains) ubiquitous; in many regions,
cannabis remained (and remains) tolerated. Widespread abstention from
alcohol had practical benefits: the negative effects of alcohol on the
health of both the individual and wider society were certainly greater than
those of the substances that replaced it. But its prohibition had a wider
symbolic function: by uniting converts to the new religion, it acted as a
social glue in a similar way to drugs themselves.

The prohibition of drugs in the twentieth century had its roots in a
similar reaction against cultural decadence. A hundred years ago, many of
today's illicit drugs were available in any high-street chemist. Cocaine was
aggressively marketed in pills, lozenges and energy drinks, or supplied
pure in solution with hypodermic needles. Cannabis was a common ingredient in tinctures and patent medicines. Bayer's new cough suppressant,

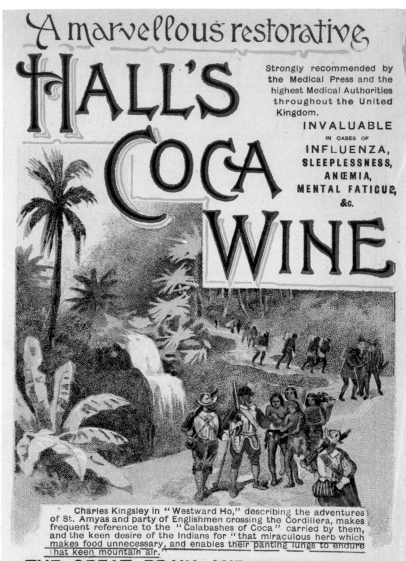

Above and right: By the end of the nineteenth century, even children's medication was laced with powerful drugs: the main active ingredient in Ayer's Cherry Pectoral (*above*) was morphine. Cocaine was available over the counter in dozens of patent preparations such as coca wines (*right*).

marketed under the brand name Heroin, was prominent among the point-of-sale displays at chemists' counters. Yet the most problematic drug, as it had been for the early followers of Islam, was alcohol. Intoxication in its traditional forms had been a constant thread through Western life since antiquity; but modern chemistry and commerce had combined to offer unbridled access to alcohol and other drugs in ever more potent forms, in ways that many believed were incompatible with the civilized society of the future.

This conflict between civilization and desire was explored at the time by the German sociologist Max Weber, whose classic work *The Protestant Ethic and the Spirit of Capitalism* first appeared in essay form in 1904. The modern West, he argued, was driven by an ethic that valorized the creation of wealth but was uncomfortable with spending it. Money was to be invested sensibly or spent modestly, rather than squandered on impulse; the ability to defer gratification was essential to social functioning, and held destructive passions in check. It was a culture, therefore, intensely concerned with the policing and management of pleasure. Alcohol, and intoxication in general, was a clear and present danger: an offence against the sovereign spirit of reason and an invitation to disorder and self-destructiveness. Yet the Protestant ethic was also producing what Weber called a 'disenchantment of the world': a society in harness to the demands of mass production, creating lives leached of pleasure and mystery, deprived of the possibility of escape or transcendence. These social contradictions were projected onto dangerous objects of consumption, such as drugs and alcohol, creating taboos around their use.

Below: Aspirin, launched by Bayer in 1899, offered a less potent and non-euphoric alternative to opiates as an everyday painkiller.

The twentieth-century prohibition of drugs, like that of alcohol under Islam, was succeeded by a culture of substitution. New substances nudged drug use away from pleasure and towards medical need. Pharmaceuticals, from aspirin to barbiturates, took over the role of opium, while amphetamines plugged the gap left by cocaine. Alcohol, after the collapse of Prohibition in the USA, was tamed by licensing and regulation. But with the consumer boom and youth counterculture of the 1960s, the mass demand for chemical re-enchantment generated yet another social form: the drug subculture.

Like drug prohibitions, drug subcultures are not a modern invention; nor do they require a legal ban before they emerge. The buzzing social network that revolved around coffee houses in eighteenth-century London, for example, was regarded by both insiders and outsiders as a drug subculture. It originated with a small but influential group whose preference for an exotic stimulant provided the motive to hive themselves

Preceding pages: In the
eighteenth-century British
coffee house, the new stimulant
drink was associated with
a distinctive subculture of
smoking, pamphleteering,
gossip and vigorous political
debate.

off from conventional society and create a new and exclusive space where
they could enjoy like-minded company. Formed in opposition to the
mainstream tavern culture of the day, it proliferated through an 'in-
crowd' of initiates and generated its own world of stimulant-fuelled
literature, subversive humour and progressive political opinions.

Traditional societies are equally capable of generating drug subcultures, particularly in times of cultural dislocation. During the 1860s, for
example, as the traditional Native American way of life was entering its
tragic and terminal decline, a 'peyote cult' spread from its traditional territory in Mexico through the tribes of the northern plains; some, but not
all, tribal members adopted and developed a ritual based around the
vision-inducing cactus. The 'cult', a synthesis of indigenous practices
with aspects of the Christian message, offered an alternative to the harsh

Opposite and below: An official of the Santo Daime church (*opposite*) brings sacramental Daime, or ayahuasca tea, to a ceremony in Brazil. During the powerful intoxication it produces, the participants pray, dance and sing hymns that were transmitted to the church's founder, Raimundo Irineu Serra, during his Daime trances (*below right*).

choice between persisting with a self-destructive warrior ethic and being absorbed into an oppressive foreign culture. It survived official persecution to become a force for stability and peace among the displaced tribes; it eventually became established as the Native American Church, and still thrives today.

The coexistence of modern and traditional cultures can also generate innovative subcultures of drug use such as the Santo Daime churches of modern Brazil, which combine Catholic forms of worship with the ritual consumption of the DMT-containing jungle brew ayahuasca. Santo Daime emerged in the 1930s from the experiences of a black rubber-tapper named Raimundo Irineu Serra who encountered ayahuasca while working among indigenous Amazon groups. His version of its rituals, based around hymns that he channelled during his visions, spread rapidly

through the working neighbourhoods of cities such as Rio de Janiero and São Paolo, where congregations now number in the tens of thousands. For the urban poor, whose parents or grandparents belonged to an indigenous jungle culture of which they themselves have no experience, Santo Daime enriches the Catholic faith with a distinctively Brazilian syncretism of African and Amerindian influences.

Drug subcultures, as in these cases, emerge as a response either to new drugs or to new social situations. Over the last half century, both of these factors have been continuously in play, and illicit drug use has proliferated across the globe. Although this subcultural explosion is unprecedented in its massive scale, global reach and aura of modernity,

Below: Ecstasy users hugging at a rave in Baltimore, Maryland, USA, in 2000. The sensitive and empathic effects of MDMA encouraged public behaviour that was quite different from the established norms of concerts and dance events where alcohol had typically been the dominant drug.

it nevertheless echoes the long-established patterns through which other cultures have assimilated drugs into their ways of life.

During the early 1980s, a new 'designer drug' emerged from a research laboratory in California and became the subject of unofficial trials among experimentally minded members of the state's large psychotherapeutic community. Word rapidly spread that methyldioxymethamphetamine, or MDMA, was a substance of exceptional therapeutic promise, and possibly even transformative potential for society as a whole. Subjects experienced waves of euphoria that made them emotionally receptive, tactile and uninhibited; in this state, they proved remarkably open to analysis and acutely empathic towards the feelings of others.

Within months, MDMA – still, at this point, a legal compound – had begun to appear alongside cannabis and cocaine on the streets, at parties and particularly in the nightclubs and discos of Texas, Chicago and New York. Its original marketers had attempted to christen it 'empathy', but 'ecstasy' emerged as a more commercial street name. Its distinctive spectrum of effects – stimulant, euphoric, empathic – made it peculiarly conducive to dancing en masse, immersed in a collective experience of brimming energy, warmth and joy. As the drug spread, so did the demand for a new type of public space. Warehouse and basement clubs with state-of-the-art sound systems and lightshows, previously the domain of gay or black subcultures, sprang up in cities across the USA and Europe; musicians and DJs surfed the chemical wave with rushing, space-age sonics and extended, hypnotic mixes. Since ecstasy was best complemented with water rather than alcohol, alcohol-licensed venues became irrelevant, and youth culture, together with its high disposable income, began to migrate away from established nightspots in city centres and into derelict industrial spaces on the edge of town, or the open fields beyond, where they could dance until dawn, or even through the whole weekend.

The intensity of the shared ecstasy experience bound its users with a powerful, initiatic sense of group identity, and expressed itself in immediately distinctive visual, conceptual and musical forms. Although much of the iconography it generated was futuristic – digital, robotic beats and dayglo plastics, with the ecstasy pill hymned as the ticket to a space voyage or a pass-key to a higher evolutionary network – many inside the culture were equally attracted by the idea that they were returning to tribal or shamanic forms of intoxication, where ecstatic dancing generated a primal engagement with nature. Imagery drawn from the DMT-inspired cultures of the Amazon proliferated across posters and CD packaging, clothing and body art, and ethnically-inflected dance mixes spawned new trance and tribal subgenres. Some underground dance collectives took to the road, travelling across Europe in a search for traditional nomadic lifeways, or migrating to the non-stop party circuits of Ibiza, Goa or Thailand. To the cultural mainstream, the phenomenon appeared terrifying: a cult that was consuming their youth in a reckless and hedonistic 'dance of death'. To its initiates, it was closer to the universal solvent represented by kava in the Pacific: at once a badge of identity, a soul medicine and a secular sacrament.

But however transcendent the experience at the heart of the ecstasy culture, it was still unfolding within the embrace of a consumer society, and as a leisure activity for those who could afford it. From the beginning, ecstasy pills had been far more expensive than comparable recreational drugs such as cannabis, amphetamines or LSD; now the big clubs were becoming vast corporate ventures, with stadium-scale sound and light shows and ticket prices to match. Top DJs were commanding staggering fees and chartering private jets to ferry them between events; designer bags and dayglo clubwear were making membership of the new tribe an expensive business while diffusing its styles far beyond the consumers of the substance. As it swept through mainstream fashion, music and media, 'e culture' exposed the tensions between the consumer ethos and wider moral messaging: the news media treated the drug as a social and medical problem, even as representations of the experience it offered were shimmering and pulsing across billboards and shop windows, televisions and computer screens. Like betel, ecstasy had become the foundation for an exuberant material culture whose scale eclipsed the drug itself.

The cultural journey of MDMA could not have been predicted either by its advocates or its enemies, not least because it came to embody so many contradictory meanings at the same time. To its initiates, it was the trigger for a chemical carnival, a form of mass intoxication without precedent; less visibly, it also developed private and therapeutic uses closer to those envisaged by its original developers. In official public discourse, it was a social evil, the spectacle of a generation prepared to risk liver damage, mental illness and even death for a night of self-indulgence; but it was also the emblem of a futuristic hedonism that insinuated itself across the youth-dominated worlds of advertising, media and commerce. It was an instantly defining symbol of modernity; but it nevertheless retraced and reinvented forms of drug culture only distantly remembered. The patterns made by drugs in human cultures may be endlessly varied, but all are perhaps woven from the same fabric.

From Apothecary to Laboratory

What is a 'drug'? In the broadest sense, it is any substance – medicine or poison – that has a biochemical effect on either mind or body. But in the particular sense of a drug that acts on the mind, the term is more contested. 'Drug', in this sense, seems not to be a neutral description but a derogatory label to be avoided. According to the industries that produce and promote them, alcohol and tobacco are not drugs; cannabis advocates claim it is not a drug but a harmless herb or a valuable medicine, and LSD enthusiasts that it is not a drug but a sacrament. Producers of coca in South America readily admit that cocaine is a drug, but maintain that its source, the coca leaf, is not: it is, rather, a revered and time-honoured element of their traditional culture. Indigenous users of substances from ayahuasca to kava to betel are appalled by the suggestion that they might be classified as 'drugs'.

Underlying the emotive connotations of the category 'drug' are two overlapping but separate understandings of the term. The first definition is purely descriptive: a drug is a substance that is psychoactive – that is, producing perceptible effects on consciousness. This is the domain of psychopharmacology, in which psychoactive drugs are classified more precisely as stimulants, sedatives, psychedelics, hypnotics, deliriants or dissociatives. In this strict sense, tea, cigars and Coca-Cola are (or, at least, contain) drugs as unambiguously as cocaine or heroin.

In popular usage, however, this clinical definition has been overshadowed by another meaning, less precise but more pervasive. Over the last century, 'drug' has come to mean a psychoactive substance that is illegal – or, perhaps more accurately, one that lacks cultural sanction for its psychoactive use. In this sense, cannabis is a drug while alcohol is not; model-airplane glue is a drug when inhaled by teenagers; khat chewed by immigrant Somali communities in the West is seen as a drug to the extent that the communities themselves are construed as a problem; and substances such as nitrous oxide or morphine are medicines when used by doctors, and drugs when used for pleasure. The classification of something as a 'drug' does not simply indicate the presence of a specific chemical substance: it is also determined by non-chemical factors such as the intention behind its use, the method of administration and the social class of the user.

Opposite: Scientists sample a strange new drug in this illustration to a fantasy tale by Aleister Crowley, published in *Idler* magazine in 1909. This was an era when new mind-altering drugs were regularly discovered by chemists, doctors and psychiatrists experimenting on themselves.

These overlaps and confusions, however, are not an exclusively modern phenomenon. The concept of a drug is an ancient one that has been compounded over time from disparate sources and traditions. It has been blurred and enriched by new substances that have emerged from global trade and scientific advances, and by the experiments of those who have investigated these substances at first hand to explore the hidden workings of the mind.

Although human engagement with drugs is effectively without a beginning, 'drug' as a concept emerged only with written history. The oldest and longest Egyptian medical text, the Ebers Papyrus, which dates from around 1600 BC, describes the roots, seeds and heads of the poppy plant; other texts suggest it was recognized as an analgesic, but it is impossible to be sure whether this effect was specifically attributed to its opium sap, or whether the plant was used, as it has apparently been since deep prehistory, for other purposes: food, medicine, incense or ritual. With the ancient Greeks, the notion of a drug came into sharper focus. Around 300 BC Theophrastus, a colleague of Aristotle, wrote two botanical treatises in which he designated certain plants as *pharmaka*, a term spanning the senses of 'drug', 'cure' and 'poison'. A comparable range of meanings survives in the English word 'intoxicant', in which concepts of altered consciousness and poisoning are similarly entwined.

Drugs, however, were a comparatively small part of medicine in the classical world. The Hippocratic tradition that emerged in the decades before Theophrastus recognized their power to act in certain conditions, but tended to assign them only a minor role in the drama of healing. The physician's art encompassed a spectrum of performance and ritual that involved not just the disease but the patient as a whole, drawing them in to perform their own cures. Medicinal drugs were catalogued and given broad characteristics, such as 'purgative' or 'emollient', but they were not magic bullets: they were suited to one type of patient rather than another, and prepared or administered in a variety of subtle ways, though most commonly stirred into oil and wine. Generalizing from one cure to another, as itinerant drug peddlers did with their wares, was regarded as ignorant and mechanistic: each patient's therapy should be a bespoke creation.

Within this framework, the category of drugs was loosely defined, and hard to extricate from other categories such as foods (the distinction is not entirely clear today: we still use prunes as a remedy for constipation, and cloves as a palliative for toothache). Plant drugs were not conceived as chemical substances contained in the root, seed or flower, but as aspects of the plant's overall personality. Modern ideas of drug chemistry and action were not sought for, or missed. Given the limited range of drugs available, and the considerable ability of good physicians to harness what is now known as the placebo effect, Hippocratic healing was a natural product of its age.

As knowledge of plants was systematized, the figure who came to be the unrivalled authority on their medical uses was Pedanius Dioscorides. Born in Asia Minor, in what is now south-eastern Turkey, shortly after the time of Christ, Dioscorides was perfectly placed to weave the disparate threads of botany and healing into the nascent discipline of pharmacy. The school of Tarsus, where he studied, had specialized in plants and medicine for generations: it was located at a crossroads, between Mediterranean Europe, Egypt and India, from where resins such as frankincense and spices such as cloves and cinnamon flowed into the West. Dioscorides' *Materia medica* listed over a thousand drugs, classified by animal, vegetable or mineral origin, together with keenly observed descriptions of what each drug 'did' and instructions on how it should be used.

It is in *Materia medica*'s fourth chapter, on medicinal roots and herbs, that we find the first descriptions of many drugs with psychoactive effects loosely grouped together. Narcotic, stimulant and depressant effects are separated, though all are discussed within the framework of pharmacology rather than pleasure ('causes sleep', 'causes frenzies' or 'eases pain'). Although he gives brief descriptions of their psychoactive effects, he is more focused on their dangers. For Dioscorides, the property that links mind-altering drugs, from the narcotic opium to the deliriant nightshades, is that they are 'cold' or 'cooling': by this he means that their effect, over increased doses, is to dull sensitivity to the outside world along a spectrum ranging from sedation or fever to sleep, and eventually to overdose and death. The leaves of the thornapple, *Datura stramonium*, for example, taken in liquid at a dose of one drachm (4 grams) produce 'not unpleasant fantasies'; but two drachms overcomes the subject completely for three days, and four drachms is fatal. It was too crude, therefore, for Dioscorides to speak of 'the effects' of a drug: its properties lie not in the substance itself but the dose at which it is taken.

Dioscorides' work remained the canonical authority on drugs for more than 1,500 years. The role of *pharmakopola*, or drug-sellers, in the classical world was taken over by the apothecaries of medieval Europe. These were seen as distinct from and inferior to physicians, who consulted in the Hippocratic manner and directed their patients to apothecaries only if drug prescriptions were needed. The remainder of the apothecary trade

Opposite and right: Dioscorides passing on his knowledge of plant drugs to a student (*opposite*), in an illustrated Turkish manuscript from the thirteenth century. His *Materia medica* remained a standard text until early modern times: this page of a German edition from 1549 (*right*) recommends the use of mandrake wine before surgical operations.

was with the general public, to whom they supplied 'simples' (mostly dried herbs) or 'Galenics', a range of standard compounds and preparations intended to rebalance the body's humours, in accord with classical medical theory.

The word 'drug' came into common English usage around AD 1400, probably derived from the Dutch term for 'dried goods', and it was also around this time that the nature of drugs began to attract the curiosity of the emerging humanists and natural philosophers. As new texts added to the store of chemical knowledge, practitioners gradually began to understand that drugs might be isolated as 'pure' substances that functioned independently of the plants that contained them, and that their effects on the mind might have a material and discoverable cause.

This process began around 1500 with the circulation of printed herbals, one of the earliest book genres to proliferate after the invention of movable type. A new edition of Dioscorides, published in 1499 and based on Greek manuscript sources that had been lost since antiquity, acted as a spur to the new learning. Herbals became more detailed and their drawings more naturalistic. Botanical gardens spread across Europe, and the first chair of botany was established at the University of Padua in 1533. By the end of the century thousands of plants had been identified, catalogued and illustrated.

The cannabis plant appears in many of these early works, though not for its psychoactive properties. European hemp, low in mind-altering cannabinoids, was mainly grown for textile production – its Latin name

Below: Illustrators at work on one of the most celebrated Renaissance herbals, De historia stirpium commentarii insignes *published in Basel by Leonhard Fuchs in 1542. In 1703, Fuchs's contribution to botany was commemorated in the name of the* Fuchsia *genus of flowering plants.*

PICTORES OPERIS,
Heinricus Füllmaurer.   Albertus Meyer.

SCVLPTOR
Vitus Rodolph. Speckle.

c diſijcit & diſſoluit. Præſens remedium eſt aphthis &
Decoctum eius tumoribus illitum eos diſſipat. Vſu
cera pudendorum, & inteſtinorum exulcerationes

DE CANNABE▸   CA

NOMINA.

χοινόϲφοφ⊙.   ANNABIΣ Græcis, Cannabis Latinis,
citur, Germanis autem Hanff.

GENERA.

Cannabis duo ſunt genera. Vna enim
φον, quod magni in uita uſus ſit ad robuſtiſsimos
mer Hanff dicitur. Altera ſylueſtris, quam Latini
wilden Hanff.

FORMA.

Satiua Cannabis   Satiua Cannabis folia fert fraxino ſimilia, grauis
Sylueſtris.   ſemen rotundum. Sylueſtris uerò uirgas fundit Al
res & minores, cubitali altitudine. Folia ſatiuæ ſim
ſubrubeos, Lychnidi ſimiles. Semen & radicem A
dere nobis nondum licuit.

LOCVS.

Satiua, in locis cultis ſata prouenit. Sylueſtris in
teſte, iuxta ſemitas & ſepes naſcitur.

TEMPVS.

Herba ad uſus medicos carpitur dum maxime u
D autore, cum maturum eſt, id quod prope autumni

TEMPERAMEN

Admodum calefacit & exiccat.

VIRES.   EX DIOSC

Satiuæ maiori copia ſumptum genituram extin
preſſus, contra aurium dolores utiliter inſtillatur
inflammationes mitigat. Tumores diſcutit, & callo
funibus utilis eſt.

EX GALEN

Cannabis ſemen flatus extinguit, adeoꝗ deſicca
ram exiccet. Sunt qui ex uiridi ſuccum exprimen
ctione, ut mihi uidetur, natos utuntur. Semen etia
quitur, ſtomacho & capiti aduerſatur, prauoſꝗ hu
facit, ideoꝗ caput æſtuoſo ac medicamentoſo halit

EX PLINI

Semen Cannabis extinguere genituram uirorv
culos aurium, & quodcunꝗ animal intrauerit, eiꝗ
taꝗ uis ei eſt, ut aquæ infuſa, coagulare dicatur, &
pota in aqua. Radix cōractos articulos emollit in a
miles impetus. Ambuſtis cruda illinitur, ſed ſæpiu

EX SYMEONE SE

Semē Cannabis comeſtum idem nocumentum
dicē enim ſi eſtur, ut illud, deliriū facit. Folia uerò
gis pro potione hæc farina exiccata, ebrietatem q
ab hauriente non ſentiatur. Apud Arabas enim p
inebriat. Deſiccat uerò ſemen genitale ut Caphura

ore serpentibus,
intertrigines, ad

LVII·

algo Canapus di-

am Grçci quumqui-
os . Germanis 3e-
uocant, Germani

s longos, inanesq,
nigriores, alpero-
& nigriora. Prioris
. Eius effigiem ui-

ris locis, Apuleiq,

autem eius, Plinio
n accidit.

li autem fuccu ex-
dix decocta alino,
ius cortex texenda

um edatur genita-
dolores ab obstru-
m difficulter conco-
. Admodum exacu-
To tentat.

fuccus ex eo germi-
olore capitis. Tan-
brum aluo fuccurri
tem podagras &c
rius quam arefca.

andrũ affert: immo
luti farina, aut uti
bitalem facit, & que
gitúrue pro uino, &

CANNABIS
SATIVA.

Zamer Hanff.
Hemp.

514

c pota, cœliaco, feminarú fluxionibus, morbo regio, & phalangiorū morsibus, &c. defl. Œdemata illius reprimit. Cortex eadem quæ fructus poteſt. Dracunculi, foliorum cum uino potum, lienem minuit. Ad dolorem dentium in deſeſsionibus. futuræ eſt, & modiorum fluxionibus in deſeſsionibus. Agitha in quibus reluit & fendùr abundanti circunfunditur. Cinis ligniorum eius appoſitæ profuſsionis ex uino hæ ſu pro poculo ininatur, quo datus in ſijs poris proſicat.

EX GALENO

Myrice prodeſt admodù lieni induratò, deiecta cum acrio uel uina rudebis, ſiue foliis, ſiue extremis ramulis. Sanat uerò etiam dentium dolores.

EX PLINIO.

Lotarus fanari ex carcinomata in uino decocta tritús cum meſſe dicit. Aſtma præcipua eſt, & fuccus eius expreſſus in uino bibitur. Adeoq mirabilibus cùm pathiam cætera folum hoc uiſcerum faciunt, ut affirment, ſic ex aluo delabit fuex, ſine liene inueniri. Et ideo homini quoque ſpleneticio chium potenti, an uaſſa ex ea faciis. Lignum & flos & folia & cortex in eoſdem uſus adhibent, quam renuſsûtur. Daráir ſanguinem hominibus cortex úrina, & comparata, feminarum, cœliacis quoçq. Idem rufus impoſitúris colletiones concenendas. Foliis exprimitur ſuccum. Ad hæc eadem & in uino decoquuntur ſanguinis eũutabilis neſſe gargenith ſtimuntur. Decoctum eorum in uino potum, uel impedimenti roſaceo & cera ſedat. Sic & epipyccidas ſanare. Ad altratium dolorem auruii, & coctum eorum ſalutare eſt. Radix ad eadem, ſimiliter & folia. Hæc meliùs quæ ſerpunt imponuntur cum polenta. Semen drachmæ pondere aduerſo língua & araneos bibitur. Cum altibium uerò pingui ſurrunculis imponitur. Hæc & & conera ſerpentium iſtus, præterquam apſidum. Necnon morbo regulino, ſiſienſibuſq decoctum infuſum prodeſt, abundantiam q mulierum ſiſtit. Lenta laboris ad omnia eadem prodeſt.

DE MECONE RHOEADE. CAP. CXCIIIℓ.

NOMINA.

Papauer rubeũ.   ηκαπ fiue Græcis, Papauer rhœas, hoc eſt, fluidum aut certù Latini, Papauer rubeum officinis & herbariis. Germani aliquii quem ludentes pueri harum folijs concaua pugno impoſita, atroq ma inciſa afoldent, ηλαπτη. & wild roen, ac Κρτορεαια appellant. Rhœas autem à flos, qui protinus decida, dictum eſt.

Κρτορεαια ab ſto Glaubðm. & wild roen.

FORMA.

Folia Eruce, aut Cichorio ſimilia, & inciſa habet, longiore ramo & ſapen Cæ ſien ũ lanigineſum, rectiuu, aſperum, cubitalem. Florem puniceum, & aliquũ candidum, ſimilem ſyluēſtria Anemones flori. Caput oblongum, minus ionæ quàm Anemones. Semen rufum. Radicem oblongam, ſubalbam, minus dig craſsitudine, amaram. Ex qua deſinatione omnibus perſpicuũ ſit, herbam quam Papauer rubeum hodie uulgò nominant, eſſe Rhœada, quod in folio Erute, lu- mato, ſuabre, & longiore: caule lanugineſo, recto, aſpero, rubinil: flore, ſipen- Anemones punicæo, nonnunquał albo, oblongo capite: ſeminiſ rufo, radice longa, ſubalbida, minoris digiti craſsitudine, guſtu amara. Errant itaqque qui Anemones eſſe arbitrantur, quod folia eius, quæ Coriandri ſint, euidenſiſsimè milquem Nos Rhœadis utriuſque picturas damus. Vnius, ætqueadeo primæ, quod Eruce folia habet, alterius quod Cichorij.

ℓ XCVI.

per terram ſparſis, iuxta folia pomis uitellis ui ſimilibus, pallida, odora. Radix fit ſemen quale pyri, radicibus magnis, binis ternúue, ſibi inuicem impli ſupericie nigris, intus candidis & craſsis cortice. Gaudem uerò non fert. Maſis folia ſunt magna, candida, lata, læuia ut Beta. Mala duplo maiora, quibus fit mox, mox odorem, cum atiqua grauitate odorata, quæ conſedentes paſtores quæ ociuntur. Radix ſupradictæ ſimilis, maior tamen candidúrq. Orba eſt ut & caule.

LOCVS

Proueſcit in iſsulis & umbroſis locis. Nunc in hortis etiam plantatur.

TEMPERAMENTVM.

Mandragora uincenitiu habet facultatem refrigeratoriam, adeò ut terti ſit or- dine frigerantum. Verunitamen nonnihil etiam caloris ineſt, & in pomis humi- tatis. Radicis cortex non tantum refrigerat, ſed & deſiccat.

VIRES. EX DIOSCORIDE.

Semen colligitur è cortice recentis radicis roſo & prælia ſubiecta, quem inſola- iti eam coteruerit, in ſiſtuli uaſk reponere oportet. Colligitur idem è pomiſ auem poruueruerunt. Delibratur radicis cortex, & trajectus lino ad uſum ſuſpen datur. Daſanit Mandragore radix in uino ad textia decoquunt, & trajecti ſp per ſeruant, utentes cyathi uniuuſ menſura in peruigiliis, & doloribus, & in quibuſue dolorũ feſsa ſecare aut urere uoluerint. Potum obſoleum duerù pom unum malù aqua Mandragore liquor, piuitam, atrægq bilem urerani mox. Venum autem copia potus uitam adimit. Miſcet medicamentis ocula- rium, & quæ dolores ſuiunt, peſsiu quoqq emolliennbus. Per ſe ſemi bola per- uiperopitum, uuncos & ſtetus trahit. Sedi pro balneo ſubſtitus ſomni facit. Ra- dix uitae oneſter ſertur, ſi ſerni horis cum eo decocta ſit, ſoin quum rubuta aliqua ferina ſit & ſcormari faciem reddere. Folia recreta, oculotú &quas ulcera exci dunt, inuunctiones cum polenta ſtira proſunt. Diſcutiunt eadem omnù duri enſiſtellas, ſtrumas, tubercula, quitoq aut ſex diebus leniter obſiccata. Vngue ad ueſtinationem deſicit. Folia condita ſale feruantur in uitem uſuin. Radix arefá- mox ex políata faciis, & ſerpentium iſtibus ex niſſe aut oleo medetur. Stra- maram tubercula, ex aqua dilitiot. Articulores dolores cum polenta ſedat. Cen- ſorum eius exciotione ſuti è cortice radicis. Teneæ minor in uina dulcæ meretú coiitunæ. Datur ex eo uerni cyathi, ſiq qui feceri, aut uel debent, ut ſerni & non coi. ſimulicio mille nunc aſsucceruerit dolore, eo quod ſomnus quundam profúi reprícẽ Rbubabdiæ, & ſomilia ſoporem afferam. Poteſt idem & eoiú fuccui. Nimiúm ta- men in olorum uſin obtureceere facit. Semen miſsilorum potum uterum purga re, confútimúq cum ſulphure ignem non expeſto rubeu feminarum profluuiâ ſiſtat, Coluguntur radix liquor, & ſcariíicata multioriarum. Per ſeſemibolù pū, in ca- canum recepta. Eſt autem liquor fucco efficacior. Sed non ſerunt omnibus locis ſaporemfeccre, idúq experientia oſtendit.

EX GALENO.

Soporem concilliandi uim habent Mandragore poma. Radicis cortex ualenfi- ſimeíꝗ: reliquum quod inius eſt imbecillium exiſtit.

EX PLINIO.

Succus fit & è malis & è caule, enciro cacumine, & radice punctis aperta aut de- roti, utila hæ cuel ſurculo. Conciſis quoque in eo ſaeolen feruatur in uino. Succus morabíq iunenire, ſed ubi pouiſ, circa uindemiæ ingenerat. Odor grauis elio, feliniq & milli gratuior. Sed iidi maturati in ſole ſiccantur. Succus exi ijs ſole denſa- tur aturo radicis nitio, uel in uino nigro ad cerulia decocta. Folia feruantur in muriis officinis, ilius recentium ſuccus peſtis noxie, ſie quoque uitæ noxie. Grauis diuem afferunt.

y 3

MANDRAGORA MAL.   Alraun mänlé. Mandroedt.

PAPAVER ER RATICVM PRIMVM.

Klapperroſen. Puppy.

supplied the term 'canvas' – though it was also held to have medical virtues, such as the use of its seeds for headaches. As the new herbal conventions established themselves through the sixteenth century, mind-altering drugs came to be grouped loosely together under the rubric of 'narcotics'. This was a category that united the opium poppy, by now well established as one of the most important remedies in the pharmacopeia, with the extensive and sinister family of intoxicant nightshades that included henbane, belladonna, datura, mandrake (mandragora), aconite (wolfsbane) and hemlock. These plants, held to be under the influence of Saturn, could be effective analgesics and sedatives but, as Dioscorides had stressed, dosage was critical: rather than aiding sleep, they might produce excitement and feverish hallucinations, or irregular heatbeats and frenzied seizures leading to heart-stopping convulsions, coma and death. Combined carefully with opium, they made a potent, if ill-starred, brew, the 'drowsy syrups' of 'poppy and mandragora' that by the time of Shakespeare's *Othello* had become proverbial agents of oblivion.

It is striking that fifteen centuries after Dioscorides, the repertoire of European plant drugs seems to have remained limited to the dark spectrum of narcotics and deliriants, all toxic and potentially fatal. It may be simply botanical accident that the rich stimulant and mind-expanding flora of the New World was absent from Europe. It is also possible that the earlier transition of the Old World peoples to settled agriculture made them less engaged with the native wild pharmacopeia than was the case for the nomadic hunter-gatherers of the Americas. Alternatively, it may be that Dioscorides' 'cold herbs' were used in Europe for their visionary properties more than documentary sources attest. But evidence for any hidden shamanic tradition is by its nature elusive, and in this case is further confused by the ways in which nightshades were invoked during the early modern witch craze, when ideas of sorcery involving sinister potions and 'flying ointments' became a central plank of the mythology of the witches' Sabbat.

Interrogated about the means by which they travelled to their Sabbat celebrations, those accused of witchcraft typically answered that they flew: on a cloak, or a broomstick, or a fork, or (most frequently) a goat. When they arrived, they ate banquets off gold and silver plates, performed blasphemous rites and backwards dances, and fornicated copiously with the Devil. The mythology of witches, broomsticks, Sabbats and flying ointments has been explained by the ingenious theory that the 'real' meaning of the witch riding her broomstick was the practice of rubbing nightshade

Opposite: Hans Baldung Grien studied under Albrecht Dürer and specialized in grotesque and erotic images of witches and supernatural scenes. In this woodcut of 1514, three witches prepare a foul potion while another flies over their heads to the Sabbat, riding on a goat.

ointments into her labia, after which she would hallucinate her Sabbat flight. But this supposition dates back only to the 1970s, and many scholars remain unconvinced that the magical ointments had any more literal reality than the claims of flight, or indeed the Devil himself. The ingredients typically listed are repetitive and formulaic, perhaps unsurprisingly, since most accounts were extracted under torture. They also include horrors such as bat's blood and baby fat, which suggest that nightshades might simply have been part of a litany of repellent and blasphemous substances. Rather than being first-hand reports of actual drug-taking practices, descriptions of flying ointments can be seen simply as magical narrative devices expected in all confessions of witchcraft.

Nevertheless, the stories of witches, ointments and Sabbats did prompt a handful of humanist philosophers, sceptical of the lurid fantasies that the witch craze generated, to attempt early experiments with mind-altering drugs and their mechanisms of action. The best known is Andrés de Laguna, physician to Pope Julius III, who in 1545 heard of a married couple who had been tortured for witchcraft and found in possession of a jar of green ointment. Laguna investigated its contents, and recognized it as a foul-smelling concoction of 'cold' narcotic herbs, with which he anointed the wife of the hangman of the city of Metz. She fell into a deep sleep for thirty-six hours, and awoke with familiar tales of attending a witches' Sabbat. He took this to prove that such devilish scenes were the product of vulgar and overheated imaginations, but also that drugs might stimulate them – or, perhaps, produce an amnesia into which they could be interpolated once consciousness was restored.

Like other sceptics of the witch crazes, Laguna did not advertise his conclusions widely; nor did his experiments add to the store of knowledge available since Dioscorides, whose *Materia medica* he translated into Spanish and cited as the authority for his conclusions. But his willingness to put drugs to the test of experiment signalled the method by which, as pharmacology came to surpass its classical authorities, the understanding of their effects on the mind would be transformed.

By this time the European category of drugs, locked in stasis since antiquity, was being expanded by global exploration. Poppies and nightshades were now augmented by the spectacular pharmacopeia of the New World: the appearance of tobacco and chocolate was accompanied by tales of the coca leaf chewed by the Indians to banish sleep and hunger, and the mushrooms that the Aztecs ate to commune with the Devil. From the Arab world came descriptions of pastes and ointments that took their subjects to fantastical worlds of beauty and terror – but also, from its alchemists

Theophraſtus Paracelſus

Medicus.

Vil zeihen mich mit argem wohn/
Als ſolt ein heimlichn Geiſt ich han/
Gottes gab all die kunſt iſt mein
Dem Menſchen zu gut bereit allein.
Starb im Jar. 1 5 4 1.

and physicians, a new chemical understanding of the essences to which the healing power of plants could be reduced. Their techniques, notably distillation, generated concentrated acids, alcohols and solvents that had the power to unlock the secrets of nature in ways thus far unimagined.

The figure who became emblematic of the quest to transform Western medicine with these new drugs and 'essences' was Theophrastus von Hohenheim, better known as Paracelsus, an itinerant Swiss alchemist and physician who gained a larger-than-life reputation from his exotic travels and outspoken criticism of classical authority. From 1517 until his death in 1541, he traversed Europe and the Near East, from Moscow to Lisbon, Oxford to Jerusalem, proclaiming that the medicine of the ancients was no longer sufficient to the modern age. In its place he offered concentrated and refined substances – vitriols, elixirs, powdered metals in distilled alcohol – which he described as 'nature fortified beyond its grade'. Some were powerful narcotics: his 'sweet oil of sulphur', apparently produced by distilling alcohol with sulphuric acid, was most likely ether, a potent intoxicant that would eventually transform surgery as an anaesthetic. Paracelsus himself noted that it sent chickens into a swooning sleep, and extinguished all pain for the duration.

Though often marginalized and ignored during his lifetime, Paracelsus's reputation grew after his death, helped by the posthumous publication of his complex and original writings and by a growing band of 'Paracelsians' who promoted his chemical therapies. Among these was laudanum, a tincture of opium in alcohol that Paracelsus had frequently hailed as a panacea, and which his followers prescribed widely for pain relief and sleep, for which it was marvellously effective. In fact, it is unclear precisely what Paracelsus's laudanum was: he seems to have used the term for several different preparations, not all containing opium, and also for a type of mastic gum more commonly known as ladanum. But opium had certainly been one of his staples, and laudanum was a fitting and effective symbol for his campaign to employ the products of nature in their most potent forms.

It was Thomas Sydenham, however, who popularized laudanum, and whose recipe would become the standard preparation. Sydenham was a physician who practised in seventeenth-century London, through civil war, fire and plague, dying shortly after the Glorious Revolution in 1689. He was known as 'the English Hippocrates' for his belief that medicine was about close observation of patients rather than dogmatic theories, but he was a Paracelsian in his conviction that there were powerful new remedies waiting to be discovered. He earned the epithet 'Opiophilos' for the regard in which he held opium: the queen of medicines, revered since antiquity, unequalled in the relief of pain, the

THOMAS SYDENHAM
Maria Beale pinxit.   *J. Houbraken sculp.*

  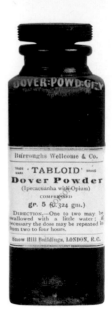

suppression of coughs and respiratory ailments, the treatment of diarrhoea and dysentery and the provision of deep and refreshing sleep. Many doctors and apothecaries mixed their own laudanums, but Sydenham's preparation was considered the best: two ounces of opium in a pint of strong red wine or port, spiced with saffron, cloves and cinnamon. For two centuries, pharmacy jars filled with this rusty tincture would be decorated in gold leaf with the motto *Laudanum Sydenhamii*.

The standardization of laudanum was a significant step in the emergence of recognizably modern drugs. Until this point, all drugs had been subject to the vagaries of nature. Their strength varied with the seasons, the habitat where the plant had grown and how it had been dried, cured and stored. From this point, in theory at least, purity and dosage were subject to human control, and each batch could be the same as the last. Standardized products could be supplied to a mass market at levels of purity and potency never before possible, and the mass market for drugs was booming. In 1732 the adventurer-turned-physician Thomas Dover, who claimed to have served an apprenticeship under the now legendary Dr Sydenham, offered to the general public a preparation even more convenient than his master's: Dover's Powder. Dover's innovation was to powder opium finely and mix it with liquorice and ipecacuana, a South American emetic, to ensure that if too much was taken inadvertently it would be vomited up rather than cause a fatal overdose.

Dover's Powder represented another conceptual leap: not simply a standardized preparation, but a commoditized product. Where Sydenham's laudanum needed to be decanted from the pharmacist's jar into the patient's bottle, Dover's product could be displayed on the shelves of any

Un Apoticaire.   Ein Apotecker.

1. vase pour la conserve de l'opiat. 1. Gefäße Medrithat auszuheben. 2. toutes sortes de boëttes à me-
decines. 2. schachtelen und Büchsen mit Arzeneyen. 3. verres à medecine. 3. Gläßlen mit Arzeneyen.
4. le sars, viperes, serpens. 4. Schlangen oder Ottern, vipern. 5. patule. 5. Spatlen. 6. ciringue. 6. Sprützen.
7. cruche. 7. ein Krügse. 8. goblet d'or à prendre medecine. 8. ein goldenes Becherl zum einnehmen. 9.
recepte. 9. recepte. 10. fourneau. 10. ein Ofen. 11. mortier. 11. der Mörser. 12. pilon. 12. der Stößel.
13. aloé. 13. aloe. 14. Simples. 14. allerley zur Arzeney dienliche Kräuter.

Cum Priv. Maj.   Mart. Engelbrecht excud. A.V.

high street grocer, already bottled up ready for purchase, complete with safety guarantee. It sold briskly, and continued to do so for centuries until it was finally removed from pharmacy shelves in the 1930s.

The eighteenth century was the great age of systematizers, and none greater than Carl Linnaeus. Around the time that Dover's Powder first appeared in British grocery stores, he was developing the system of botanical classification that would gradually become the modern standard, and through which his name has been immortalized. Yet this was only the beginning for 'God's registrar', as he called himself, a man born with a sacred mission to describe and catalogue nature in all its forms. In 1749 he published his *Materia medica*, tabulating the names and synonyms of all known medicinal plants, their countries of origin and habitats, the techniques for their preservation and their doses and pharmaceutical effects. In 1753 he finally completed his *Species plantarum*, a two-volume work that described over 8,000 plants in unprecedented detail; and in 1762, during the final phase of his life as the presiding genius of the University of Uppsala in his native Sweden, among monographs on everything from lemmings to leprosy, ants to electrotherapy, he published a

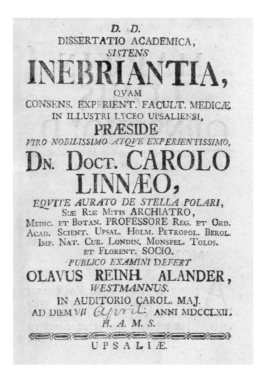

Opposite: Carl Linnaeus in the traditional dress of the Sami people of Lapland, whom he visited during his first major scientific expedition at the age of twenty-five.

Right: Linnaeus's *Inebriantia*, published in 1762, was the first recognizably modern taxonomy of mind-altering drugs.

Above: A seventeenth-century etching of Circe, identified as a sorceress by her magic book and wand, who has just turned Odysseus's crew into beasts. For Linnaeus and his contemporaries, this episode from *The Odyssey* could be read as a cautionary tale about the power of drugs to rob men of their reason.

short work entitled *Inebriantia*, the first recognizably modern inventory of mind-altering drugs.

Its first modern contribution, signalled on the title page, is a clear definition of the substances in question. By 'inebriants' Linnaeus refers not to all drugs, but specifically to 'those stimulants which affect the nervous system in such a way that there is a change not only in its motor but in its sensory functions': essentially the definition of psychoactive or consciousness-altering drugs still used in pharmacology today. Although he admitted frankly that there was as yet no satisfying physiological explanation for how these drugs worked, he was beginning to notice structural commonalities between them. Most of them, for example, had a bitter taste, a property that would be explained by the alkaloid chemistry of the century to come.

Inebriantia was also modern in its global scope. In addition to the familiar European flora of poppies and nightshades, Linnaeus presented many drugs from the East: preparations of cannabis including Turkish hashish pills or the Persian drink known as bangue; the seeds of the Syrian rue, *Peganum harmala*, now known to contain the same alkaloids as the ayahuasca vine of the Amazon; even the combination of betel leaf, areca nut and lime from the far Orient. The drugs of the New World, such as tobacco, were also represented and Linnaeus had previously written monographs on coffee, tea and chocolate. With this global perspective, he was able to observe that 'almost no nations are without intoxicants'. The familiar European triumvirate of alcohol, poppy and nightshade could now, for the first time, be compared with and situated among a wealth of exotic alternatives.

In other respects, however, Linnaeus's work strikes the modern reader as curious. Drugs are classified into three types: natural, artificial (alcohol, especially distilled spirits), and mythical. In the last, the drugs of classical antiquity such as nectar, nepenthes and moly are considered as methodically as the rest, with their properties carefully enumerated. Linnaeus also turns to mythology to describe the effects of drugs. The reader is presented with the image of an old man to whom successive drinks are offered by magical figures such as Medea; each one takes him back further through the seven ages of life, the correct dose restoring him to his prime before an overdose reduces him to a helpless infant. This image is Linnaeus's grand metaphor for the action of stimulants and sedatives: their powers over the nervous system allow us to speed up and slow down our metabolisms, and thereby change our bodies instantly from old to young through chemical means.

Other classical myths illustrate the dangers of drugs in the *Inebriantia*. The sorceress Circe, whose potion reduced Odysseus's men to beasts, stands as a timeless warning of the mental and physical degradation to which the uncontrolled appetite for intoxication can lead. Linnaeus's particular focus was on distilled liquor: he had spent much time botanizing in the wild north of Europe, where he had frequently been appalled by the excessive spirit-drinking he witnessed in remote villages. Several of his students, too, had succumbed to alcoholic excess. Within the newly discovered global cornucopia of drugs, strong alcohol seemed to him by far the most destructive. He was suspicious of coffee, which in his opinion drained vigour and induced early senility, but he was a heavy smoker, and recommended tobacco as a weapon against infection.

Linnaeus's exhaustive catalogue of drugs would, however, soon be out of date. The passion for classification that he epitomized was continuing to expand the list: most conspicuously via global exploration, but also by closer inspection of Europe's indigenous flora. On 3 October 1799, a doctor named Everard Brande was summoned to the London home of a poor family who were in the grip of a mysterious and perhaps fatal toxic crisis. The father, whom Brande identified only as 'J. S.', had begun the day in his customary fashion in the autumn by going down to Green Park at dawn to gather small field mushrooms, which he brought back and cooked up 'with the common additions' – flour, water and salt –

in an iron saucepan to make a morning broth for his wife and four children. But an hour or so after their breakfast the family began to suffer strange and alarming symptoms. 'J. S.' developed vertigo, losing his balance, black spots spreading across his vision; the rest of the family complained of poisoning, their stomachs cramping and extremities becoming cold. He left the house to summon help, but within a few hundred yards was found in a confused state, having already forgotten where he was going and why, and the doctor was called.

By the time Dr Brande arrived, the family's symptoms were rising and falling in giddy waves. He noted their pulses and breathing intensifying and fading, periodically almost returning to normal before launching into another crisis. All of them were seized with the idea that they were dying, except for the eight-year-old son, Edward, whose symptoms were the strangest of all. Edward had eaten a large portion of the mushrooms and 'was attacked with fits of immoderate laughter', from which neither the threats of his father or mother could restrain him. Between laughing fits he exhibited 'a great degree of stupor, from which he was roused by being called or shaken, but immediately relapsed'. The pupils of his staring eyes were the size of saucers, and he would speak only nonsense: 'when roused and interrogated as to it, he answered indifferently, yes, or no, as he did to every other question, evidently without any relation to what was asked'. Dr Brande treated these bizarre and frightening symptoms with emetics and fortifying tonics, and it was to these that the family's recovery was attributed when they returned to normality several hours later. Brande regarded the incident as exceptional enough to write a full description for the *Medical and Physical Journal*, on the grounds that these 'deleterious effects of a very common species of agaric, not hitherto suspected to be poisonous' should be made known to doctors and public alike.

The history of the liberty cap or 'magic' mushroom in Britain and Europe is, like that of the nightshades, a contested one. By analogy with other cultures, particularly those of the Americas, knowledge of its hallucinogenic effects might be presumed to date back into prehistory, but the proof for this remains elusive, and there is much suggestive evidence to the contrary. In Dioscorides and the early herbals that followed him, fungi were regarded as a single species with some edible forms, but essentially putrid and unhealthy. There are scattered early references to toadstools that cause delirium, and Brande's is not the first report of an accidental intoxication; there was a generalized understanding that some mushrooms might cause hallucinations, but this was taken as simply another example of their well-known poisonous nature. Given that the liberty cap is one small mushroom among many species that fruit in the same conditions, and its effects are not noticeable unless several are ingested

Opposite: These are the mushrooms identified by James Sowerby in his four-volume *Coloured Plates of English Fungi* (Vol. III, 1803) as responsible for the intoxication witnessed by Everard Brande. As indicated by the pencil marks on this copy, the three small peak-capped specimens on the right appear to be liberty caps (*Psilocybe semilanceata*), but the remainder are more likely to be *Stropharia* species, commonly known as dung roundheads, which often grow alongside liberty caps but have no hallucinogenic properties.

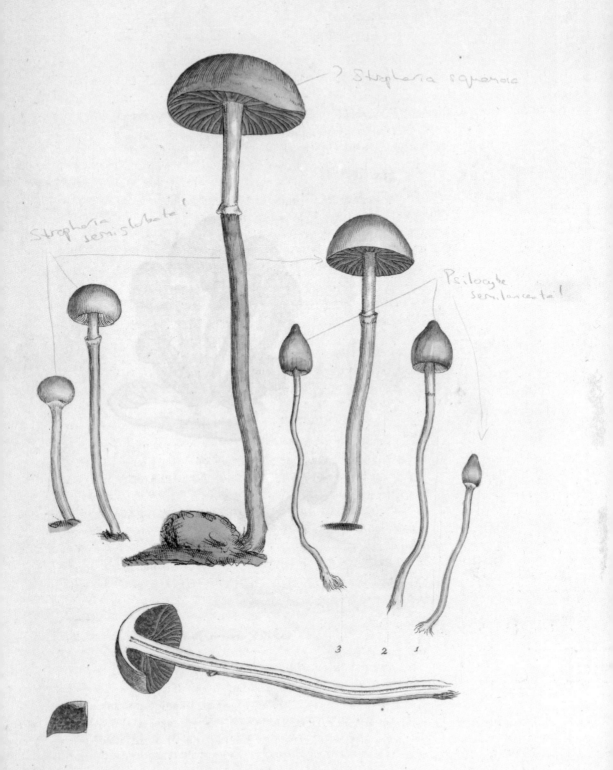

? Stropharia squarrosa

Stropharia semiglobata?

Psilocybe semilanceata?

3   2   1

Feb 1. 1802. Published by J. Sowerby London

Agaricus semiglobatus

squarrosus?

together, it is entirely possible that its distinctive properties were not recognized until modern times.

Brande, too, was unaware of the exact species of mushroom that had caused the family's symptoms, but in the scientific climate of the Enlightenment such details were now being scrutinized more closely. His account of the incident caught the attention of the botanical artist James Sowerby, who was just completing an illustrated guide to English fungi and delayed publication to include an illustration of the small mushrooms he suspected to be responsible. During the nineteenth century, however, Sowerby's identification was forgotten: the liberty cap was confused with other species and its hallucinogenic properties conflated with those of the far more distinctive red-and-white fly agaric (*Amanita muscaria*), whose use by Siberian shamans was becoming known in the West through the accounts of Polish and Russian travellers. The psychedelic counterculture of the 1960s unfolded in ignorance that the liberty cap was a hallucinogen. It was not until the late 1960s that Brande's mushroom was conclusively identified as *Psilocybe semilanceata*, a European native species containing the recently discovered alkaloid psilocybin, and matched to Sowerby's plate, and only in the early 1970s that 'magic mushrooms' were incorporated into modern drug culture.

During the same year in which Brande recorded the effects of the liberty cap mushroom, another new drug was inadvertently discovered, under very different circumstances and with more dramatic consequences. Throughout the spring and summer of 1799, a remarkable group of experimental subjects had been deliberately dosing themselves with a substance that was not only a new chemical, but a new state of intoxicating matter: gas. At the Pneumatic Institution in Hotwells, a spa town on the outskirts of Bristol, they had synthesized nitrous oxide, inhaled it, and discovered to their astonishment that it altered consciousness in dramatic and unforeseen ways. Their reports would present this new state of mind to the world in unprecedented detail, and would earn nitrous oxide its enduring nickname of 'laughing gas'.

The Pneumatic Institution was the brainchild of Thomas Beddoes, a physician of dazzling erudition and energy who was gripped by the conviction that a revolution in drug therapies was long overdue. Chemistry, he argued, had been transformed by the likes of Joseph Priestley and Antoine Lavoisier, who had deconstructed nature into its primary components and revealed its secret structures, but medicine remained a backwater of gentle Hippocratic therapies and time-honoured herbal panaceas. His particular preoccupation was diseases of the lung, such as

Right: Thomas Beddoes (1760–1808) was convinced that new drugs and chemical therapies had the potential to transform the antiquated medical profession of his day. His experiments on gases led to the discovery of nitrous oxide, and the first experiments with a synthetic mind-altering substance.

Following pages: Humphry Davy (1778–1829), originally hired by Beddoes as a laboratory assistant, made his name with the daring and original experiments he performed to study the effects of nitrous oxide, and was offered a prestigious post at the Royal Institution in London. In this cartoon by James Gillray from 1801, Davy is shown operating the bellows while his distinguished audience samples the gas.

consumption, that by his estimates were killing one in four British adults. The new gases such as oxygen, discovered in 1774, offered the novel possibility of treating the lungs directly. Beddoes decided to devote his energies to establishing a combined laboratory and clinic where gases could be made and tried on invalid patients.

In the late eighteenth century, Beddoes's conviction that chemistry was poised to transform the art of medicine was not widely shared. Pure chemicals were still associated with the kill-or-cure doses of acids and toxic metals favoured by the followers of Paracelsus, and seen as desperate remedies of last resort. Medicine was dominated by tradition rather than experiment, and the idea of testing new remedies on the sick was fraught with ethical concerns. The Pneumatic Institution was viewed with suspicion before it opened, but the course of its experiments proved even more alarming than anticipated. Beddoes had hired as his assistant a brilliant, young self-taught chemist named Humphry Davy, who made rapid progress in synthesizing new combinations of gases and testing them on himself. Within a month of its launch, he made the discovery for which the Institute would become famous, and notorious. Inhaling nitrous oxide from an oiled silk bag, he began to notice 'a highly pleasurable thrilling in the chest and extremities' that, as he breathed harder, swelled to a crescendo of overwhelming sensations that left him shouting for joy and leaping around the laboratory.

S! — or — an Experimental Lecture on the Powers of Air —

Beddoes and Davy appreciated immediately that this was a discovery with revolutionary implications. An artificial gas, unknown in nature, was being absorbed through the lungs and immediately overwhelming the nervous system, surpassing the potency of any chemical medicine thus far imagined. Beddoes inhaled the gas, noting its euphoric and restorative effects; Davy, enthusiastic and ambitious, began to take heroic doses, and to extend the trials to other subjects. Beddoes's social circle in Bristol included a vibrant coterie of physicians, poets, philosophers and political radicals, among them the young Romantic poets Robert Southey and Samuel Taylor Coleridge. Together they began an exuberant and free-wheeling series of experiments in which they attempted to describe nitrous oxide's effects.

It rapidly became clear that this was a project that had never been attempted before, and for which the ground rules needed to be established from scratch. Davy was testing the gas on rabbits, kittens and fish, noting its effects on respiration and heartbeat, and measuring how much of it was absorbed into the bloodstream; but animals could not report on their sensations, let alone their thoughts. If there was to be a science of mind-altering drugs, its protocols would need to include human experiment, and specifically self-experiment by the researcher himself.

The barrier that the experiments faced was language. There was no adequate vocabulary for these hitherto unexplored states of mind: as one of the researchers put it, 'we must either invent new terms to express these new and peculiar sensations, or attach new ideas to old ones, before we can communicate intelligibly with each other on the operations of this extraordinary gas'. What was required was 'a language of feeling', as Davy called it: a project that the Romantic poets were also engaged in constructing. Chemistry had opened the door to this new discipline, but it could not answer all the questions it raised. The tools of poetry, and of philosophy, were required to make sense of the drug's action on the mind. Pushing his experiments to the limit, Davy eventually concluded that 'nothing exists but thoughts': reality itself was constructed in the mind, from the data relayed by the senses. Nitrous oxide, by hijacking the sensory inputs to the mind, had the effect of transporting the subject to a new world.

For Thomas Beddoes, the discovery of nitrous oxide was a transformative moment for medicine, and for humanity itself. He and Davy had discovered a chemical that seemed to produce happiness on demand, the harbinger of a future where new discoveries might free mankind from the age-old tyranny of the body and allow it 'to rule over the causes of pain and pleasure'. But this idea was still fiercely resisted on religious and moral grounds, and Beddoes's utopian dreams were ridiculed in press

LIVING MADE EASY.

LAUGHING
GAS

GAS

PRESCRIPTION FOR SCOLDING WIVES.

London. Pub.ᵈ by T.M°Lean, 26, Haymarket. Jan 1. 1830.

Above: Nitrous oxide was largely ignored by the medical profession, but was eagerly taken up in public entertainments where it acquired its enduring nickname of 'laughing gas'. There were many ingenious suggestions for its possible applications, such as this etching from 1830.

and public. It would be half a century before nitrous oxide's defining application, anaesthesia, would transform medicine by permitting pain-free surgery.

Yet Beddoes's belief that new chemicals would give humanity unprecedented control over pain and pleasure would soon be vindicated. In 1803 a young German pharmacist's apprentice named Friedrich Sertürner began experimenting with a tarry opium concentrate, attempting to reduce it to its acidic components. Over many years he produced a number of obscure substances, which he tested on himself and others. Eventually, in 1817, he isolated a compound that formed clear crystals soluble in acid, though only slightly soluble in water. He enlisted three teenage boys to drink a solution of the crystals with him in cautious half-grain increments, but the drug was far stronger than he had anticipated. He and his subjects suffered violent vomiting fits and fell into a heavy stupor, from which they were only revived by drinking strong vinegar. Sertürner christened his extract morphine, after Morpheus, the Roman god of sleep.

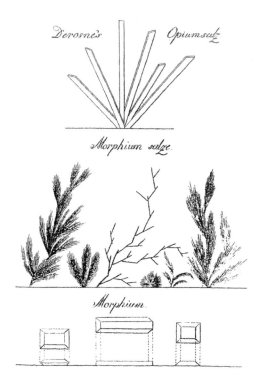

Right: A plate from Friedrich Sertürner's paper of 1817, 'Über das Morphium', illustrating the crystalline forms of morphium salts. His discovery galvanized chemists to search for other plant compounds that could be extracted as pure crystals and trialled as medicinal drugs.

This was the first time that a plant had given up not merely an essence or a tincture, but a pure chemical substance in its own right, and Sertürner made several observations that laid the framework for the isolation of pharmaceutical plant extracts. Having painfully established over a decade that these active components were not acids, as he and others had assumed, he classed them as 'vegetable alkali' (later to be known as alkaloids). He also established that crystallization was the best way to isolate them and, once isolated, to keep them free from contamination by other substances. These discoveries would transform chemistry, particularly in Germany, into an industrial science supplying new plant-derived compounds to a vast pharmaceutical market. Caffeine would be isolated from coffee in 1820, and nicotine from tobacco in 1828. In 1832 an entirely separate substance, codeine, would be found alongside morphine in the juice of the poppy head. In 1842 chocolate would be discovered to contain a unique psychoactive drug, theobromine, and in 1860 the coca leaf would yield the most powerful, and lucrative, stimulant yet: cocaine.

The practice of self-experimentation in science was not unique to Beddoes, Davy and Sertürner. In an era when human trials were widely seen as unethical, many breakthroughs in biology and medicine had been made by researchers who had treated their own bodies as laboratories.

The discovery of digestive juices, for example, had been announced in 1780 by the great Italian physiologist Lazzaro Spallanzani, who had observed their action by swallowing and regurgitating linen bags at varying time intervals. But psychoactive drugs demanded self-experimentation for a different reason. The data they sought was not physical but subjective: changes of mood or perception, the sensations of anxiety or ecstasy, the stimulation of insights and epiphanies. Could these unverifiable reports be scientific data in the first place? Yet if they were excluded, how could the effects of these drugs be studied?

As the nitrous oxide researches had shown, this was a form of experiment that demanded more than the usual scientific skills. Literary and creative gifts could be at least as valuable, and the inward turn of pharmacology was being paralleled in the arts by what would later become known as the Romantic movement. Samuel Taylor Coleridge, for example, had participated in the nitrous oxide trials, and his personal testimony of a state 'of more unmingled pleasure than I had ever before experienced' had been included in Davy's clinical report. Coleridge's notebooks from the period are filled with exquisite observations of his states of mind: speculations about their origins in bodily sensations or the natural world around him, incidents that might have unconsciously influenced them, and memories that emerged unexpectedly to illuminate them. In a sense, he was making his entire life into a self-experiment, from which he generated reports in the form of poetry, psychology and philosophy.

Below: Black Drop, the potent brand of laudanum used by Samuel Taylor Coleridge and Thomas De Quincey during their residences in the Lake District. This bottle is now displayed in Dove Cottage in Grasmere, which De Quincey and his family rented for twenty-five years after taking over the lease from William Wordsworth in 1809.

It was shortly after his encounter with nitrous oxide that Coleridge moved to the Lake District and became seriously dependent on opium (in the form of Kendal's Black Drop, a patent preparation notoriously more potent than *Laudanum Sydenhamii*). His addiction arose partly from medical use for symptoms such as headaches, and nervous conditions such as anxiety and insomnia; it then became deeply woven into the condition of his life, not least as a furtive and guilty pleasure. While most of his references to opium are as a poison that has destroyed his health and sanity, others suggest that his early use, at least, was driven by the urge to explore what he described, in a letter to his brother George in 1798, as a 'divine repose...a spot of enchantment, a green spot of fountains, & flowers and trees, in the very heart of a waste of sands'. Those closest to him recognized the shining eyes and glowing cheeks that indicated he had taken a generous dose, and knew that its power lay behind his most eloquent dinner-party performances, but his drug habit was also an acute source of private shame and misery, which he only confessed to once it was no longer possible to conceal it. In modern parlance, drug use is separated with confident precision into 'medical' and 'recreational'; Coleridge's career is a reminder of how recent this distinction is, and of how blurred it can become.

It was Coleridge's protégé Thomas De Quincey, however, whose name would become synonymous with the Romantic fascination with opium. His *Confessions of an English Opium Eater*, published as a serial in the *London Magazine* in 1821 and as a book in 1822, was an immediate sensation that marks the arrival in popular culture of drugs as agents of pleasure and fascination, sought out and indulged in by a subculture of bohemian connoisseurs, bringing exquisite sensations or soul-destroying agonies – or, as in De Quincey's case, both. Where Coleridge had attempted to keep his drug use from public view, his erstwhile secretary took the opposite route by making his addiction to opium the central fact of a fractured and hallucinatory narrative of his life.

The image of the drug user that De Quincey constructed would shape public perceptions for the rest of the century and beyond. Laudanum was a familiar, even mundane product, by this time available from any general store and often cheaper than alcohol, but the pleasures it afforded De Quincey were mysterious and sublime. Opium, he insisted, does not intoxicate in the clumsy manner of alcohol; rather, it brings a profound sense of order to the conscious mind, allowing it to explore its own hidden byways and secret passages, to examine the construction of its own thoughts and memories, until 'the moral affections are in a state of cloudless serenity; and over all is the great light of the majestic intellect'. As its title subtly indicates, the true subject of his book is not the drug but the opium eater himself, who has penetrated its mysteries to grasp 'the doctrine of the true church on the subject of opium: of which church I acknowledge myself to be the only member'.

The pains of opium, however, were more than equal to its pleasures. Like Coleridge, De Quincey's habit developed along familiar lines: early use of the drug for pain relief (later recalled as the golden moments of bliss that baited the trap) was followed by several years of occasional and pleasurable excursions before escalating into dependency, in which the drug offered short-term relief at the price of a progressive enslavement, trapping him on a nightmarish treadmill of sickness, insomnia, night terrors, debt and dependency. The drug that had promised to relieve the condition had itself become the condition: dozens, sometimes hundreds of grains were required to keep the horror at bay, forcing him ever deeper into the heart of the labyrinth, and face to face with the monstrous and distorted selves that hid in the darkest recesses of his soul.

Confessions of an English Opium Eater set a moral template for the public presentation of drug use that would endure, and that continues to proliferate in modern-day tabloid 'My Drug Hell' confessionals. It insisted that the pleasures of drugs, however voluptuous, were ultimately barren: they might be cheaply purchased, but their true cost was one than no man

Opposite: Thomas De Quincey's status as the archetypal 'drug fiend' continues to resonate in modern popular culture, as in this film from 1962 – even though the narrative has been transposed to late nineteenth-century San Francisco, and the protagonist's bottle of laudanum anachronistically replaced with an opium pipe.

could afford to pay. Yet this morality play can also be seen as a literary device, another twist in De Quincey's artful self-dramatization. Opium was his curse, but it was also the crutch that enabled him to endure the self-inflicted chaos of his lifestyle, for which it was both the cause and the excuse. 'The Opium Eater' would remain De Quincey's epithet for the rest of his remarkably long life. It was a living death, but it was also immortality.

De Quincey's public self-experiment was richly spiced with solipsism and self-delusion, but it also yielded valuable clinical insights into the nature of addiction. Doctors were relying ever more heavily on Sydenham's 'queen of medicines', with little attention to the consequences of its prolonged use. It was understood that regular laudanum users needed to increase their doses, but this was generally seen as a minor side effect of an indispensible remedy, and most doctors were more concerned by the risk of accidental overdose, a more conspicuous cause of fatality. De Quincey was scathing about the ignorance and misinformation surrounding opium within the medical profession, and countered it with his acute observations of the ways in which the drug insinuated itself into mind and body through the mechanisms of craving, tolerance, dependency and withdrawal.

De Quincey's example demonstrated that self-experimentation could not only lead to the discovery of new drugs but could also transform the understanding of ones that had been known and used for centuries. Over the next generation, the same spirit, part scientific and part Romantic, would stimulate the enduring modern fascination with two more plant intoxicants, one from the Orient and the other from the New World: cannabis and cocaine.

Although the European cannabis, or hemp, plant was weak in psychoactive chemicals, it had been known for some time that the subtropical strains of the same plant acted as a powerful intoxicant in the Arab world and Asia. Linnaeus had identified Turkish *maslac* and Persian *bangue* as preparations of *Cannabis sativa* from those regions, and the tales of delirious hashish-eaters in the *Arabian Nights* were widely known in translation. It was assumed that the plant had different forms in hot climates, although some speculated that the drug it contained only worked on the less well-developed Arab nervous system.

In fact, some Europeans had experimented successfully with cannabis: the sea-captain Thomas Bowrey had tried *bhang*, a traditional drink of cannabis buds steeped in milk, with his crew on a voyage to Bengal in 1689, but his diary account of his subsequent derangement was

Opposite: A hashish market in Cairo, in a chromolithograph published in Paris in 1850. The psychiatrist Jacques-Joseph Moreau de Tours purchased some *dawamesc* – hashish mixed with sugar and spices – during his visit to Egypt in 1836, and his reports of his experiment with it inspired a bohemian fascination with the exotic drug.

never published. Napoleon's troops became familiar with hashish during their occupation of Egypt in 1800, but the first to give a detailed account of its effects was a young psychiatrist from Paris, Jacques-Joseph Moreau de Tours, who embarked in 1836 on a three-year journey to Egypt accompanying a wealthy patient on a rest-cure. He had been curious to investigate the relatively low prevalence of insanity in the Arab world compared to Europe, and on his arrival was struck by a suggestive difference: the lack of alcohol, and the widespread use of cannabis. On his return to Paris, he brought some samples of *dawamesc* or hashish, the bitter greenish paste made from the fresh plant's resin and sweetened with sugar and spices, and one evening swallowed a dose of three grams before dinner. Its effects began while he was eating oysters, and reduced him to helpless fits

of laughter; by the time he found himself preparing to fight a duel with a bowl of candied fruit, he recognized that the hallucinatory tales of the *Arabian Nights* had a firm foundation in reality.

These properties of hashish held a particular interest for Moreau, who specialized in the study of monomania and hallucination and their relation to 'normal' mental states. He recognized immediately that the abnormal phenomena he was attempting to study in his insane patients – errors of time and space, *idées fixes*, delusions of poisoning – were now available to him at first hand. The insight challenged his views of insanity: patients apparently in a dull, semi-conscious stupor might in fact be in the throes of mania, with thoughts and ideas flying around their brains too fast to express them. Self-experimentation was, he realized, essential. 'I

Below: A group of women lounge in an oriental setting in *L'Haschisch* ('Hashish Smokers'), an oil painting from 1887 by the Italian pointillist Gaetano Previati.

" HE DISTINCTLY SAW WITHIN HIMSELF THE DRUG HE HAD CHEWED."

Above and opposite below: Hashish visions became a familiar element in the decadent, oriental and symbolist aesthetic of the late nineteenth century. In this comic engraving (*opposite below*) a Romantic writer seeks inspiration by smoking it. An article entitled 'Haschisch Hallucinations', a collection of famous literary accounts of experiences under the influence of hashish, was published in the *Strand Magazine* in 1905, and illustrated by the visionary artist Sydney Sime (*above*).

Opposite above: Among the early experimenters with hashish was Jean-Martin Charcot, a pioneering neurologist and mentor to Sigmund Freud. Charcot took the drug as a medical student in 1853, and experienced 'a tumult of phantasmogoric visions', which he attempted to capture in this sketch.

Above: Théophile Gautier, author of the narrative *Le Club des Haschischins*, in an early daguerrotype portrait by the photographer, balloonist and revolutionary Nadar (Félix Tournachon) (top). Gautier also penned this sketch of Jacques-Joseph Moreau de Tours, playing the piano in Turkish dress under the influence of hashish (*above*).

challenge the right of anyone to discuss the effects of hashish', he wrote, 'if he is not speaking for himself'. Here was a drug that not only demonstrated a chemical basis for insanity but also allowed psychiatrists to experience a safe and temporary facsimile of it for themselves.

Like Beddoes and Davy with nitrous oxide, Moreau was interested in testing his new drug not only on the sick but on artists and *littérateurs*, who were also becoming interested in attempting to communicate its effects in poetry, painting or philosophy. He and a fellow doctor, Louis Aubert-Roche, who had also spent time in the Orient and had proposed hashish as a specific against the plague, joined a literary circle that met monthly in the Hôtel Pimodan, on the Île Saint-Louis in the centre of Paris, in rooms furnished in lavish Oriental style for evening salons known as the Club des Haschischins. Before dinner, the city's bohemian *demi-monde* were served large oral doses of hashish, which plunged them into several hours of intense delirium. If nineteenth-century accounts of cannabis seem overwrought to modern readers, at least part of the reason is the extravagant quantities in which it was consumed.

The most celebrated account of the Club, by Théophile Gautier, was published in the *Revue des deux mondes* in 1846. Gautier admitted later in life that he had indulged the gothic and fantastical fashion of the day and his account of the event was wildly mythologized, but it still gives a vivid sense of the tone in which the experiments were conducted. 'Doctor X' welcomes the guests in a Turkish robe and turban, spooning a smear of green paste onto an elegant Japanese saucer with a ritual admonition: 'this will be deducted from your share in Paradise'. Guests wearing long beards, medieval poignards and Oriental daggers gather for a feast; as it progresses, they begin to notice an exquisite confusion of the senses, their meat tasting of strawberries and vice versa. At the cry of 'To the salon!', the guests – in Gautier's account, now transformed into menacing masked apparitions with owl eyes and beaked noses – withdraw to a huge gilded room decorated with painted satyrs, where music plays and the revels descend into Goyaesque delirium until the drug fades, time and reality are reinstated, and the shell-shocked initiate finds his midnight carriage waiting for him in the street outside.

If Thomas De Quincey became a prototype for the modern 'drug fiend', the Club des Haschischins prefigured the 'drug scene' of the century to come, with its instantly recognizable leitmotifs of long hair, late hours, radical politics, free love and insatiable curiosity about exotic substances. It generated the most extensive canon of drug literature to date: its familiar roll-call of alleged members includes Honoré de Balzac (who wrote in 1846 of his urge to make 'a study upon myself of this very extraordinary phenomenon'), Gérard de Nerval (who later wrote tales of hashish set in Egypt), Alexandre Dumas (whose Count of Monte Cristo is dosed with green hashish jam on a desert island) and Gustave Flaubert (whose projected novel *La Spirale* was to feature a hashish-eating painter reduced to madness). But its most exacting account of hashish intoxication came from Charles Baudelaire, who in 1851 published a long essay on drugs entitled 'Du Vin et du haschisch'.

Baudelaire admired De Quincey's *Confessions* as the finest work ever written on opium, and his own account of hashish followed in the Opium-Eater's footsteps, with the drug making its subject a god before casting him into hell. His description of the 'seraphim theatre' of hashish separates the intoxication into three finely observed stages: the nervous

Right: A self-portrait by Charles Baudelaire made under the influence of hashish. Baudelaire rented rooms in the Hôtel Pimodan, where the gatherings of the Club des Haschischins were held, but according to Gautier only tried hashish 'once or twice by way of experiment'.

thrill and 'giddy cheer' of its onset, the overpowering sensory cavalcade of its peak and the oceanic calm tinged with melancholy in its wake. But the show, he insists, comes at a terrible cost, and the soul-sickness of the morning after reveals the true nature of the 'forbidden game' into which hashish lures the user by gratifying his 'natural depravity'. Baudelaire took hashish infrequently – perhaps no more than once – and his verdict on it perhaps bears the imprint of his more considerable experience with opium; but his account set an influential template for the tormented drug confession in French literature, just as De Quincey had done in English.

As in the case of hashish, the discovery of cocaine was set in motion by the self-experiments of a curious physician posted to a foreign destination. Paolo Mantegazza was a young Italian doctor who spent four years practising in Argentina in the mid-1850s, during which he encountered coca-chewing Indians and tried the leaves himself. Having found coca leaves agreeable as an evening tonic, he proceeded to chew as much as possible to test their effects to the limit. His book *On the Hygenic and Medical Values of Coca*, published in 1859, described the plant's power to increase muscular action, remove hunger and fatigue and, at high doses, to produce a thrilling mental excitement and stimulate rapid-fire speech. Intrigued by Mantegazza's account, the University of Göttingen requested a sample, and in 1860 the young chemist Alfred Niemann was presented with 25 kilos of coca leaf shipped from Lima, from which he produced a white crystalline alkaloid that he christened 'cocaïne'.

Niemann died within a year, and his work was largely ignored. As one of many recently isolated alkaloids, and with the potency of the coca plant still unproven because so many samples arrived from South America spoiled, cocaine languished on the laboratory shelf for twenty years. In the interim, however, coca wines and tonics became popular pick-me-ups, and in 1883 a German army doctor, Theodor Aschenbrandt, acquired a sample of the pure alkaloid and tried adding it to the water he supplied his Bavarian recruits. He observed an increase in stamina, and recorded his hopes that soldiers might use the drug to dispense with food and sleep for extended periods, even as long as a week. The following year his paper came to the attention of another self-experimenting doctor, a young Viennese neurologist named Sigmund Freud, who followed its references back to the work of Mantegazza and ordered his own sample of the drug from the Merck pharmaceutical company in Darmstadt, who listed it in their exhaustive catalogue of research chemicals.

Freud, swallowing doses of a tenth of a gram dissolved in water, immediately noted 'a sudden exhilaration and a feeling of ease', and

Below: During his research into cocaine, the young Sigmund Freud, studying under Jean-Martin Charcot in Paris, was sometimes obliged to attend formal dinners that made him shy and nervous. In letters to his fiancée, Martha, he confessed to dosing himself with small amounts of cocaine to supply confidence and 'untie my tongue'.

Above: Traditional coca farming in the Andes, in an engraving from 1867. Traces of coca have been found in 3,000-year-old mummies, and the leaf has been widely cultivated and chewed across the region for at least 1,500 years.

suspected that he had made a significant discovery. The nineteenth-century pharmacopeia was becoming relatively rich in sedatives – new synthetics such as chloral hydrate were by now widely used alongside morphine and opium – but there were no stimulants more effective than the old standbys of tobacco, alcohol, tea or coffee. Alert to the danger that self-experiment might slide into self-deception, Freud proceeded to establish that his feelings of increased energy were not all in his mind by measuring his muscular force with a dynamometer, and showing objectively that cocaine increased it. He published his findings in 1884 in a paper entitled 'Über Coca', his clinical reportage spiced with exuberant language intended to convey the sensations the drug imparted. Cocaine was a 'gift' from nature that produced 'the most gorgeous excitement', not merely a stimulant but a mood elevator that reliably produced 'exhilaration and lasting euphoria'.

As Freud's career progressed and the public image of cocaine took a darker turn, 'Über Coca' would become a hostage to fortune, used by his opponents to blacken his reputation for the remainder of his life and beyond. With hindsight, its glaring omission is its failure to mention the addictive properties of the drug, and the dangers of repeated high doses. Many blamed Freud's reckless self-experimentation for his rosy view of cocaine; but perhaps his experiments were too cautious. After a small dose, he confessed, he felt nothing but 'a slight revulsion' at the idea of taking more, but larger doses would have revealed the less benign effects of the drug. At the time, however, Freud's most obvious tactical blunder was his failure to capitalize on cocaine's most promising medical application, as a local anaesthetic in eye surgery. The credit went to his Viennese colleague Carl Koller, who had noticed its numbing qualities when Freud first presented him with a dose.

Freud's portrayal of cocaine as an agent of pleasure, even an aphrodisiac, did his reputation no favours, but it did no harm to the reputation of cocaine, which rapidly became integral to the great pharmaceutical boom of the late nineteenth century. Since the 1870s coca had been a popular ingredient in tonic wines, sweetened pick-me-ups that in 1891 came to include Coca-Cola, advertised as a 'nervine tonic' and a cure for 'hysteria, headaches and melancholia'. By that time, however, far stronger forms of cocaine were being heavily marketed by the major pharmaceutical companies Merck and Parke-Davis: the pure alkaloid in powder or solution, along with a range of convenient preparations that included throat lozenges, tablets and toothache drops, and even impregnated bandages, cigars and cheroots. As part of its product range, Parke-Davis also supplied hypodermic kits in smart pocket-sized steel cases together with cocaine, morphine and miniature needles. Their catalogues promoted the drug as a panacea that 'can supply the place of food, make the coward brave, the silent eloquent'. Cocaine had become the perfect product: it could be sold as a remedy for almost any condition, with the confident assumption that the customer would very likely feel better after using it.

By 1890 high street pharmacies had become places of wonder. With pioneers such as Burroughs Wellcome now producing exquisitely machined tablets in all the colours of the rainbow, their shelves were compared to sweet shops. Among this exotic pharmacopeia, opium, cocaine and cannabis, the three plant drugs that would become the mainstays of the twentieth-century's illicit trade, were all well represented. Cannabis was the least prominent of the three – then as now, it proved hard to produce in standardized pills and extracts – but it was nevertheless regarded as a useful specific for a range of complaints including insomnia, migraines and muscle spasms. It was a favourite remedy of Queen Victoria's physician John Russell Reynolds, who described it in *The Lancet* in 1890 as 'one of the most valuable medicines we possess', and may have prescribed it to the monarch for stomach cramps or childbirth.

Although the illicit substances of today were becoming familiar, the modern stigma-bearing notion of 'drugs' was yet to emerge. Cocaine,

Opposite: Coca wines and tonics were pioneered by the Corsican pharmacist Angelo Mariani, whose 'Vin Mariani' – coca leaves steeped in sweetened burgundy – became a mass-market product, endorsed by several European monarchs, an American president and two popes. By the 1890s there were many rival brands across Europe and the United States, including, from 1891, Coca-Cola.

SAVAR'S COCA WINE

The restorative and tonic properties of Coca are well exhibited in wine, but most Coca Wines are weak in Cocaine.

SAVAR'S COCA WINE, manufactured in our own laboratories, is standardised to contain half-grain Pure Cocaine per fluid ounce, and being of this strength it is classed as a true medicated wine.

N.B.—A 4s. 6d. bottle contains ten fluid ounces; in 2 drachm doses, this would last a patient about a fortnight; a 7s. bottle contains 20 ounces.

EVANS SONS LESCHER & WEBB,
LIMITED,

60, BARTHOLOMEW CLOSE, LONDON
AND
56, HANOVER STREET, LIVERPOOL.

Above: A late nineteenth-century pharmacy in Kensington, London. By this time the traditional range of manufactured soaps, syrups and patent extracts had been joined by enticingly packaged tabloids and pills, many of them containing morphine or cocaine.

opiates and cannabis were culturally sanctioned in the sense that they were on open sale; at the same time, the idea of a Club des Haschischins-style plunge into chemical insanity still appealed to no more than a handful of bohemians. When Arthur Conan Doyle gave his detective hero Sherlock Holmes a cocaine-injecting habit in 1890, it sat intriguingly alongside his violin, meerschaum pipe and metropolitan bachelor lair to denote a highly strung and eccentric sophisticate. But by the end of the century, Doyle would be scaling back his hero's habit, of which Dr Watson had disapproved from the first. The image of such drugs was changing fast, not least because of the new and shocking form of administration favoured by Holmes himself: hypodermic injection.

Originally developed for treating local infections, by the 1880s the hypodermic needle was widely used in medicine, particularly for morphine. The combination of powerful narcotic and subcutaneous injection revolutionized acute care by offering a release from pain that was almost instant and almost total. But its overwhelming wave of euphoria and relief from stress and care was, for some, too good to confine to emergencies. Although most of the early 'morphinomaniacs' were nurses, doctors and their spouses, needles were also on sale in pharmacies to the general public, and commonly supplied to military officers. By the 1890s they had acquired a recognized class of problem customers, most of whom had first encountered hypodermic needles in a therapeutic context but had continued using them with no thought for health or sanity, frantically pursuing an escalating desire for morphine or cocaine or both. Terms such as 'drug inebriate' were coined by analogy with the more familiar phenomenon of alcoholism, and 'drug addict' and 'narcomaniac' rapidly migrated from the medical literature into common parlance.

At this point, however, the line between 'medical' and 'recreational' use was still difficult to draw. Late nineteenth-century doctors were struggling to cope with an epidemic of nervous complaints whose natures were obscure, but were clearly related to the stresses and anxieties of industrialized modern life. Diseases such as 'neuralgia', which encompassed a wide range of symptoms from repetitive strains to panic attacks, and 'neurasthenia', a constitutional weakness that could lead to physical or mental collapse, were increasingly treated with powerful stimulants and sedatives, a range that now included opium, morphine, bromides, sulphonal, cocaine and chloroform (one popular compound, chlorodyne, contained morphine, ether, chloroform and cannabis). But those with nervous diseases were also the most likely to succumb to the new categories of drug addiction. It was hard to designate drugs themselves as the problem when they were also being promoted to the public at large as the solution.

By the beginning of the twentieth century, the 'drug menace' was the target of medical and media campaigns, and drugs themselves were spreading from the pharmacies and clinics to become more visible on the streets. There had long been concerns that the working classes might be doping themselves with opium, not as a medicine but as a cheap alternative to drinking themselves into oblivion. These concerns were heightened by the spread of Chinatowns across America and Europe, and the fear that the Chinese habit of smoking opium for pleasure might spread through the docks and inner cities. In America, servicemen demobbed from the Spanish–American conflict were forming gangs in tenderloin districts of the port cities, and sniffing cocaine in bars and pool halls; in the South, cocaine, opium and morphine were circulating among the black community in jazz dives and red-light districts. In New York, addicts who sold scrap to feed their habits were becoming known as 'junkies'; in the cities of Europe, where cocaine and morphine had disappeared from the pharmacy shelves, street-corner hustlers in the theatre and pleasure districts were selling them in paper packets. The public image of the drug user was changing from medical patient to dangerous thrill-seeker. In the process, the term 'drug' was acquiring its modern meaning.

After a succession of international trade acts and state regulations, the American Harrison Narcotics Tax Act of 1914 eventually codified the

Above: A stylishly designed hypodermic syringe set, nickel-plated brass in an aluminium case, marketed by the pharmaceutical company Parke-Davis in the 1890s. This example was owned by the surgeon Sir Frederick Treves, remembered for his friendship with Joseph Merrick, the 'Elephant Man'.

Below: The combination of hypodermic injection and powerful synthetic drugs led to an increase in cases of 'narcomania', or drug addiction. This plate from a medical textbook of 1881 shows a male nurse whose habit of self-injection has covered his body with abscesses.

Right and opposite: Eugène-Samuel Grasset's 1897 painting *Morphinomaniac (right)* captures the subject's frenzied mix of excitement and desperation, while the image of a cocaine addict losing his mind (*opposite*) labels the drug a scourge of humanity.

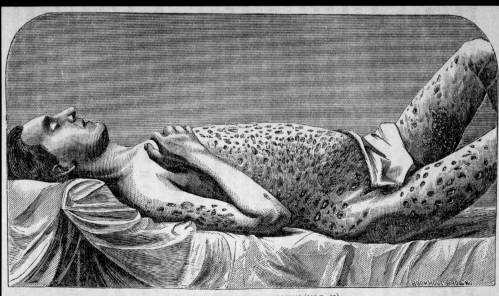

RESULT OF SUBCUTANEOUS INJECTION (see p. 71).

La cocaïne, fléau mondial

Illustration de Henri Gazan

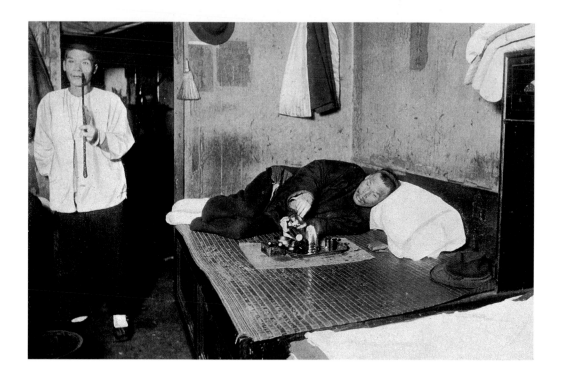

Above: An opium den in San Francisco's Chinatown in the early 1900s. At that time the Chinese community in San Francisco was the largest in the Western world. Opium dens were prohibited by a city ordinance of 1875, but they continued to operate clandestinely until the Second World War.

ongoing process of removing opiates and cocaine from the shelves by forcing all suppliers to register with the government, and limiting their sales to official medical use. It was the Harrison Act that introduced 'narcotic' as a medico-legal term for all illegal drugs, whether strictly narcotics or (like cocaine) stimulants. Similar laws were enacted as wartime emergency measures across Europe in the years that followed, and later adapted into permanent prohibitions.

The practical consequence of these controls was to accelerate a search for substitute drugs that was already underway. In 1898 the German chemical giant Bayer had produced a morphine substitute, diacetylmorphine, which they had marketed as a cough suppressant and cure for morphine addiction under the brand name of Heroin. As a 'narcotic', it was withdrawn after 1914; but by now Bayer had plenty of new products to plug the gap. In 1899 they had launched Aspirin, which had taken a large share of the headache pill market to which opiates had previously catered; in 1903 they had produced Veronal, the first commercially available barbiturate and prototype for a class of strong sedatives that would take over morphine and chloral's roles in medicating the casualties of modern life. Veronal's inventor, Joseph von Mering, was said to have named it after the city of Verona, the most peaceful place he knew.

Right and below: In the years after the First World War, morphine and cocaine were widely available, especially in cosmopolitan cities. A magazine illustration from the 1920s depicts the fashionable demimonde of cocaine use in Weimar Germany (*right*); during the same period a Berlin street dealer sells capsules of cocaine while his partner keeps a lookout in the background (*below*).

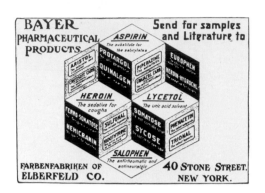
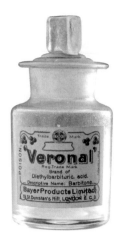

Right and far right: By 1900 the Bayer pharmaceutical range included both Heroin, a powerful new variant on morphine, and Aspirin, an opiate-free analgesic (*right*). Veronal, launched by Bayer in 1903, represented a new category of sedatives, the barbiturates, which would be marketed as a less addictive alternative to opiates (*far right*).

A substitute was also found for cocaine's stimulant effects. Since the 1880s, chemists had been investigating the alkaloids of the ephedra plant, widely used across Asia as a herbal stimulant, and in 1927 the British pharmacologist Gordon Alles synthesized a derivative that he named amphetamine. He experimented on himself and noted a marked stimulant effect, after which the new drug began to circulate around the medical profession. William Sargant, a psychiatrist at London's Maudsley Hospital, took a powerful dose before wandering around the zoo 'with a most delightful sense of confidence and not in the least fatigued'; he took more before sitting his diploma examination, and passed with flying colours. He tested it on depressives, and found that their moods temporarily lifted; he even established that it improved their scores in intelligence tests. Less markedly euphoric than cocaine and longer-acting, amphetamine had great therapeutic potential, but also functional benefits for the sane and healthy.

Amphetamines found their first major application during the Second World War, when they were used to boost the endurance of soldiers and pilots in combat. Thereafter, they became a popular over-the-counter pharmaceutical, marketed for mood elevation, energy and 'pep', but it was not long before their open sale began to acquire the taint that had attached to opiates and cocaine. William Sargant was appalled that such a valuable energy and intelligence booster had become 'a source of cheap "kicks"' for 'psychopaths, drug addicts and simple delinquents'. In Britain, as elsewhere, their sale was more strictly regulated; yet, as with valium and the other sedatives that were emerging at the same time to replace the cruder barbiturates, they remained hybrid substances, valued therapeutic agents and stigmatized 'drugs' simultaneously. Once laws were in place to define legitimate therapeutic applications, a clear distinction could in theory be made between 'medical' and 'recreational' use, or 'use' and 'abuse'. In practice, however, modern societies would continue

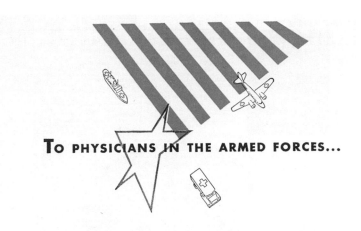

To physicians in the armed forces...

All last winter physicians in the Armed Forces kept writing us for their "usual" BENZEDRINE INHALERS. ★ Evidently, under Service conditions—the most exacting test of practical usefulness—Benzedrine Inhaler demonstrated its unique combination of convenience and therapeutic effectiveness. ★ So we hope that any Army or Navy physician who wishes a Benzedrine Inhaler for his personal use, will return the coupon below or drop us a postcard. (We have no other way of obtaining your address.) ★ Smith, Kline & French Laboratories, 107 N. Fifth St., Philadelphia 5, Pa.

BENZEDRINE INHALER

A VOLATILE VASOCONSTRICTOR

In the new plastic tube...

Each tube is packed with racemic amphetamine, S.K.F., 250 mg.; oil of lavender, 75 mg.; and menthol, 25 mg. Benzedrine is S.K.F.'s trademark, Reg. U. S. Pat. Off.

SMITH, KLINE & FRENCH LABORATORIES, 107 N. FIFTH STREET, PHILADELPHIA 5, PA.

In accordance with your offer to physicians in the Armed Forces, please send me one of your new plastic BENZEDRINE INHALERS.

Name_____

Address_____

to require a wide spectrum of culturally sanctioned stimulants and sedatives, and their citizens would continue to demand them for reasons that blurred the boundaries between therapy and pleasure, 'feeling good' and 'feeling better'.

But the chemistry of the twentieth century had far more spectacular mind-altering drugs in store than 'uppers' and 'downers'. The harbinger of these was mescaline, the hallucinogenic alkaloid of the peyote cactus, which native Mexican peoples had been taking for sacramental purposes since prehistoric times and which had spread north during the nineteenth century as old tribal structures were disrupted. James Mooney, a young ethnographer from the Smithsonian Institution who was studying the Ghost Dance movement that had arisen among the Sioux tribes in 1890,

Right and below: The mescaline-containing peyote cactus (*right*) was adopted as a sacrament in the late nineteenth century by many Native American groups, such as the Comanche, whose peyote ceremony (*below*) was photographed by the ethnographer James Mooney in Oklahoma in 1892.

became the first white man to be initiated into its mysteries. Seated around a sagebrush fire in a tepee in a circle of braves, painted and feathered and in their finest buckskin, he chewed and swallowed four peyote buttons, and noted their 'especially wonderful mental effects'. After a night of drumming and chanting, Mooney was asked to 'go back and tell the whites that the Indians had a religion of their own which they loved'.

The 'discovery' of peyote, however, was rapidly claimed for science, and the race to discover its active ingredient began immediately. The only substance known at the time to produce powerful hallucinogenic effects lasting several hours was hashish, but the self-experimenting chemist Arthur Heffter of the University of Leipzig eventually isolated a new crystalline substance that he named after 'mescal', as the peyote plant was then known to cactologists. During the 1890s mescaline was dubbed 'a new artificial paradise', and was explored from many different angles. Pharmacists trialled it as a heart stimulant and a nerve tonic; the leading American psychiatrist Silas Weir Mitchell experimented with it as an aid to psychotherapy; and the British sexologist and art critic Havelock Ellis compared its effects on perception to Maori wood-carving and arabesque tapestry, the painting of Monet and the poetry of Wordsworth.

Despite the contemporary panics over opiates and cocaine, mescaline was not regarded as a 'drug' but a research chemical, and it was added to the Parke-Davis catalogue without controls. Although it never found a therapeutic application, it continued to be of interest to psychologists studying perception and cognition, and to artists of the modernist avant-garde such as Henri Michaux and Stanisław Witkiewicz, who used it to induce fertile states of creative derangement. It was in this self-experimental tradition that Aldous Huxley produced the most celebrated work of mescaline reportage, Doors of Perception, in 1954; but by this time another far more potent hallucinogen had emerged from the Sandoz laboratories in Basel, Switzerland. On 19 April 1943 Albert Hofmann, a chemist reserching derivatives of the ergot fungus in the search for a vasoconstrictor to treat haemmorhages, took a tiny experimental dose of lysergic acid diethylamide, and within an hour found himself experiencing violent changes in perception. He headed for home on a bicycle, but by the time he arrived the world had transformed entirely, dissolving into a flux of kaleidoscopic spirals and fountains.

LSD, as it became known, was a focus of intense interest in a post-war world where 'psychotropic' medications such as lithium were promising a radical expansion of drug therapies for depression and other mood disorders. Psychotherapists reported the astonishing progress made with long sessions of analysis under its influence, during which patients could unlock deeply buried traumas and gain an empowering

Opposite: Albert Hofmann, the discoverer of LSD, is commemorated in the celebrated 'blotter art' of Wes Black. The image is printed across a sheet of tiny perforated squares of blotting paper, the form in which doses of LSD are commonly produced for the illicit market.

sense of perspective on their lives. But, as its use spread, it became clear that similar benefits could also be experienced by those who were not ill or under medical supervision. Particularly in California, where therapy mingled with the cults of Hollywood celebrity and radical self-improvement, LSD began to be promoted as an experience that would add richness to the life of anyone who chose to take it. As it diffused into the emerging counterculture, it made a rapid transit from research chemical to 'drug', and when the Sandoz patent expired in 1963 it became a controlled substance. Mescaline followed soon after, with the Native American Church eventually winning a hard-fought legal exclusion to permit their religious use of the peyote cactus.

But the prohibition of LSD and mescaline could not obscure the chemical vistas their discovery had opened up. Both, it had become clear, were representatives of large families of related substances, with effects on consciousness thus far entirely unknown. Among those exploring this terra incognita was a Californian biochemist named Alexander Shulgin. He had developed profitable pesticides for the Dow Chemical Company, and had been given the freedom to research new psychopharmacology compounds, working with the Drug Enforcement Agency (DEA), for whom he would perform chemical assays on samples and appear in court as an expert witness. In 1965 Shulgin left Dow to become an independent researcher, working out of a private laboratory in the hills outside San Francisco with a DEA licence to manufacture scheduled drugs.

Shulgin recognized that the phenethlyamines – the family of drugs to which mescaline belonged – formed a continuum with the ampheta-mines, and that there were hundreds of intermediates that might combine the hallucinogenic effects of the former with the euphoric and stimulant effects of the latter. It emerged that one of these compounds, methyldioxymethamphetamine (MDMA), had been synthesized by Merck in Germany as far back as 1912, but had never been tested. He developed a new synthesis, and in 1976 began producing the substance that would soon be known as ecstasy. Thereafter Shulgin's laboratory became the birthplace of hundreds of new compounds, their chemical formulae abbreviated to an alphabet soup of names such as 2C-B, DOM and 2C-T-7. It also became the focus for a discreet network of self-experimenters who tested the effects of the new compounds, taking them in carefully recorded doses and publishing their findings anonymously.

Shulgin spent his early career testing laboratory drugs on animals in the conventional manner, but regards the need for self-experimentation with psychoactive drugs as 'obvious to anyone who gives the matter some thought'. Each new substance that emerges from the laboratory is a tabula rasa: its effect on human consciousness cannot be predicted simply from

its chemical structure. Although the DEA has attempted to curtail his work since he published his research notes and syntheses in two doorstopping volumes, Shulgin continues to publish, and to unfold new psychopharmaceutical vistas. In recent years he has pioneered the synthesis of 'fly' and 'dragonfly' compounds – wing-like extensions to the molecular structure that create new and more potent variations on his already vast repertoire. The permutations may be, to all practical purposes, infinite.

Like Augustus Owsley Stanley III, the underground chemist who distributed an estimated five million doses of LSD in mid-1960s San Francisco, Alexander Shulgin has become the flamboyant figurehead for an invisible army of illicit drug manufacturers. The search for mind-altering drugs has split into two streams, overground and underground, but the two have continued to inform one another, and may do so more intimately in the future. Since the 1990s, dubbed by President George H. W. Bush the 'decade of the brain', a 'neurotransmitter revolution' has expanded the scope of psychotropic medicine, and signalled the possibility of drugs

Right: Alexander 'Sasha' Shulgin in his laboratory in northern California, where he has synthesized hundreds of previously unknown mind-altering compounds and recorded their effects at varying doses along a self-devised scale: 'plus one' (noticeably psychoactive), 'plus two' (effects marked, but still controllable), 'plus three' (fully immersive) or 'plus four' (a transcendental, 'peak' experience).

Above: Staff at Fagron Pharmaceuticals in the Netherlands pack cannabis that has been grown and licensed for medical use. This type of clinically regulated procedure, along with hi-tech pharmaceutical preparations such as inhalant sprays, has helped to shift the image of the plant from stigmatized drug to modern pharmaceutical medicine.

that might make patients not only well, but 'better than well'. Cutting-edge 'smart drugs', 'nootropics' and mood enhancers – from cognitive stimulants such as piracetam to attention boosters such as Modafinil – promise improved brain function and memory, even heightened levels of creativity and wellbeing.

Taking these predictions to their logical conclusion, some commentators claim that we are on the brink of a future posthuman condition where brains are chemically tuned to their optimum level of performance, all anxiety and dysfunction is medicated away and heightened consciousness becomes a permanent, even universal state. In this brave new world of neuro-enchancement, what would become of our modern concept of a 'drug'? Perhaps the digital and networking devices in which we now cocoon ourselves might even evolve to stimulate our neurochemistry directly, without the need for illegal substances. If so, might the enhanced descendants of our iPods become 'drugs'?

Whether or not such predictions are plausible, they reflect the feeling that the twentieth century's carefully constructed boundaries between 'medical' and 'recreational' cannot be permanent. Drugs such as Prozac and Ritalin edge medicine towards the neurochemistry of ecstasy and amphetamines; illicit drugs such as cannabis are losing their social stigma and making their way into the medical pharmacopeia; new disorders pathologize states that were once regarded as normal, such as anxiety or low self-esteem, opening the door to the medical use of drugs that boost confidence and happiness. The category of 'drugs' can never be entirely fixed, determined as it is not only by chemistry but by society. In a future where drugs evolve to stimulate the brain with ever more precision, perhaps the most enduring distinction will remain the one formulated by Dioscorides 2,000 years ago: whether a drug is medicine or poison is a question of dosage.

The Drugs Trade

One of the many curious sights witnessed by Christopher Columbus and his crew on their first landing in the New World was that of two Taíno Indians rolling dried leaves into large cigars, lighting them and inhaling the smoke. When questioned, they told the Spaniards that the plant's name was *tabaco*. It was a sight that was to become familiar to the explorers, conquistadors, colonists and traders who followed Columbus. Tobacco, in its various forms, turned out to play a central role in American cultures from Canada to Chile, California to Brazil. Some smoked it, some chewed it, some snuffed it from carved wooden trays, some drank a black and bitter concentrate of its juices. It was used for healing, for purifying, for hospitality, for treaty-making between tribes, for engaging with the spirit world, and simply for sociability and enjoyment.

Tobacco was part of a constellation of even more mysterious intoxicating plants in the New World. The Jesuit priest José de Acosta, who resided in Mexico in the sixteenth century, witnessed Aztec priests grinding its leaves together with poisonous hairy caterpillars and the seeds of a plant known locally as *ololiuqui* to make a drink that caused them to see visions – or, as he interpreted it, to 'become witches' and communicate with the Devil. The brew, according to Acosta, did indeed possess supernatural powers: it enabled the priests to heal the sick, to divine the whereabouts of lost articles and even to predict the future. He believed the natives to be innocent of evil, but it was clear that the Devil was taking advantage of their innocence: why else would he mock them by forcing them to participate in a gross parody of the Eucharist? The Europeans who first encountered the potent visionary medicines of the New World projected onto them two warring tendencies from within their own culture: a thirst to expand their medical knowledge, and a profound suspicion that these plants were imbued with diabolical powers.

Ololiuqui, a flowering creeper of the morning glory family, contains in its seeds the closest natural analogue to LSD. It was not the only powerful hallucinogen in use among the Aztecs. They were also in the habit of eating a mushroom they called *teonanácatl*, meaning 'flesh of the gods' in their Náhuatl tongue, which drove them into a visionary frenzy where they would dance, sing, weep and hallucinate until the intoxication passed, at which point they would sit together and discuss their experiences. Other Mexican peoples venerated a cactus that they would consume on

Opposite: A Turk drinking coffee, a Chinese man drinking tea, and an Aztec drinking chocolate, each from its distinctive pot, in a French engraving from 1688. The spread of new plant commodities, especially stimulant drugs, after the discovery of the New World was central to the emergence of global trade.

occasions such as harvest ceremonies, sitting in a circle and playing music as its effects took hold before dancing for hours, even days, in a shuffling trance. They knew this cactus as *peyote*; the Jesuits called it 'the Devil's root'. Getting the Indians to grasp that these plants were diabolical turned out to be one of the most difficult doctrinal points in their conversion. 'The people venerate these plants so much', José de Acosta recorded, 'that they do all in their power so that their use does not come to the attention of the ecclesiastical authorities.' Many Indian groups, once converted, simply gave saints' names to the intoxicants and continued to use them in their liturgies.

Yet there was no denying that the 'savages' had great medical knowledge. They maintained botanical gardens for their healing plants, and the people traded a vast range of remedies in their markets. From Hernán Cortés onwards, many conquistadors had found native treatments for wounds and local diseases more effective than European ones. Tobacco,

Right: A sixteenth-century Aztec statue of Xochipilli, the Prince of Flowers, in an ecstatic trance. The stylized flower glyphs on his body include the tobacco plant, the morning glory and the deliriant *sinicuichi*; the buttons on his plinth represent the hallucinogenic mushroom *teonanácatl* (*Psilocybe aztecorum*).

Opposite: A Huichol man collects peyote in San Luis Potosí state, Mexico. Isolated in their rugged mountain homeland of the Sierra Madre Occidental, the Huichol people are among the few Mexican groups whose traditional beliefs have survived with little Catholic influence. Their annual 300-mile pilgrimage to gather peyote has persisted largely unchanged since pre-Columbian times.

revered by so many Indian peoples, had piqued their curiosity from the first contact: Rodrigo de Jerez, one of Columbus's crew who had witnessed the Taíno use of *tabaco*, had himself become a regular smoker, and on his return to Spain was imprisoned by the Inquisition for the devilish practice of exhaling smoke through his mouth and nose. But by the time he was freed, many more had taken up the habit. Unlike the hallucinogenic cacti or mushrooms, tobacco was a 'safe' intoxicant that caused no loss of sense or decorum, and could be detached from its diabolic native rituals and incorporated into the European pharmacopoeia.

Travellers' tales and plant samples were fed back to Europe from the early expeditions, and by 1550 the first tobacco plants were growing in Dutch herb gardens. But it was a Spanish physician, Nicolás Bautista Monardes, who provided the most influential account of the new plant discoveries. His books, published in Spanish between 1565 and 1574, created a sensation and were swiftly translated into Italian, French and German, and in 1577 printed in English as a single volume entitled *Joyfull*

Above: Early Spanish explorers
witness a South American
ceremony in which the chief
smokes tobacco in a long pipe
while his people shake maracas.
Relics of other indigenous
groups, such as this bas-relief
sculpture of a Mayan priest
smoking a cigar, attest to older
traditions of tobacco use in
the Americas (*right*).

Newes out of the New-Found Worlde. Monardes was the first to describe the coca plant, regularly used by the natives of the Andes to suppress hunger and thirst while they worked, and chewed together with tobacco when they wished to 'go out of their wittes'. He also revealed the existence of cocoa and medicinal herbs such as sarsaparilla and sassafras; but it was tobacco that formed the centrepiece of his discoveries. Monardes' description of it, and of its many medical uses, sparked an obsession with the 'holy herb' that would prove to be the first manifestation of a global drug culture.

Monardes had gathered his 'joyfull newes' without making the voyage to America in person. He had requested plant specimens from adventurers and grown them in his botanical garden in Seville, observing their development carefully and making sample preparations from them. Some travelled better than others: had coca leaves maintained their potency on the long voyage or thrived in the European climate, the world might be drinking them alongside tea and coffee today. But tobacco, in Monardes' opinion, was the most miraculous of the new plants. He classified it in terms of the Galenic humours as 'hot' and 'dry', an astringent and a purifier, a purgative for a system that had become cold or lethargic and a specific against diseases of the cold and damp such as asthma or catarrh. Although these virtues were contained in the smoke, the plant was equally useful in other forms: it could be chewed to treat stomach ailments, and the leaves applied topically for headaches. He described the native habit of using it as an intoxicant with disapproval, though several of his prescriptions seem to have been borrowed from reports of Amerindian practices.

The practice of smoking announced the novelty of the New World drugs as much as tobacco itself. It had no precedent in European culture, and was initially described as 'drinking smoke' or 'fog-drinking', by analogy with alcohol. Opinion was sharply divided: some hailed smoking as the proof of a new age of wonders, others as a sign that the world was descending into barbarism. Many were receptive to Monardes' claims that tobacco was a panacea, and that its astringent smoke warded off diseases and foul airs, but it was opposed with equal vehemence, most famously by King James I, whose *Counterblaste to Tobacco* of 1604 characterized it as an unhygienic habit spread by the vain and foolish. But the medical debate was only a prelude to its wider use. During the seventeenth century, as Europeans learnt to appreciate its stimulant and euphoric properties, it became a familiar part of daily life.

The habit spread via travellers and traders, and especially soldiers. In a life of male companionship that alternated between long periods of boredom and short bursts of extreme stress, it proved to be just what

Opposite: An illustration of the tobacco plant from a 1580 Spanish edition of Nicolás Monardes' medical treatises on New World plants, works that greatly influenced the early spread of tobacco in Europe.

❧SEGVNDAPARTE❧

Del Libro, delas cosas que se traen de nuestras Indias Occidentales, que siruen al vso de medicina. Do se trata del Tabaco, y dela Sassafras, y del Carlo santo: y de otras muchas Yeruas, y Plantas, Simientes, y Licores: que nueuamente han venido de aquellas partes, de grandes virtudes, y marauillosos efetos.

¶ *Hecho por el Doctor Monardes: Medico de Seuilla.*

EL TA- **BACO.**

Los

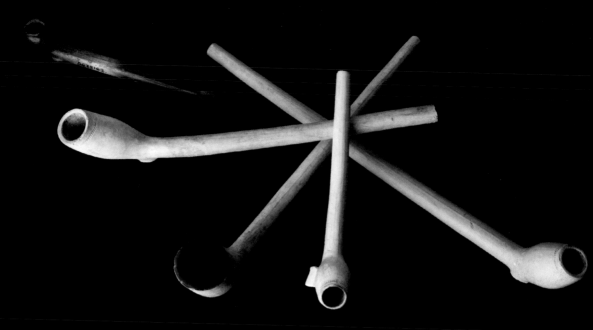

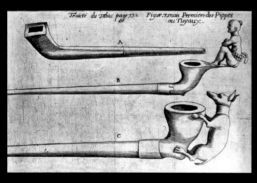

Top: Clay pipes from sixteenth-
and seventeenth-century
London, where similar examples
can still be found on the
foreshore of the Thames at
low tide.

Above: Pipe designs from the
Americas, in an engraving from
Johann Neander's *Traicté du
tabac*, published in Lyon in 1626.

Right and opposite: A Dutch
apothecary relaxing with a pipe
in a 1646 painting by Adriaen
van Ostade (*right*). Tobacco was
frequently seen as an aid to
contemplation, producing a
state of mind in which thoughts

could drift freely, like smoke.
Equally, it was an aid to
sociability, as for this gallant
Londoner-about-town depicted
in a woodcut from 1620
(*opposite*), who, with his
'smokinge pipe', intends to
'singe, dance, drinke, and
merrily passe the day'.

MULLD:SAKE.

I walke the Strand, and Weſtminſter,and ſcorne ⎱ My ſmokinge Pipe, Scarfe,Garter,Roſe on ſhoe.
to march i th' Cittie,though I beare the Horne. ⎰ ſhowe my braue minde t' affect what Gallants doe.
My Feather, and my yellow Band accord ⎱ I ſinge, dance,drinke, and merrily paſſe the day,
to proue me Courtier. My Boote,Spurr, and ⎰ and like a Chimney ſweepe all care away.
ſword

Are to be ſold by Compton Holland, over againſt the exchange

the doctor ordered. The Thirty Years' War spread it from the Atlantic seaboard across central and eastern Europe (just as, two centuries later, the Crimean War would play a similar role in popularizing the modern cigarette). First in ports and cities, then through market towns and the countryside, 'smoke-drinking' became a congenial accessory to moments of leisure and companionship. The practice was concentrated in taverns, where men would smoke as an accompaniment to intoxication just as the Indians did, using devices adapted to European taste and supplied by European manufacturers. Initially pipes were formed in the American style, with small bowls that were passed around and shared; but from around 1620 a distinctive local form had emerged, with a larger bowl and often a foot-rest, designed for individual use. This proliferated in a variety of materials: filigreed silver for a noble, clay for an urban worker, or a simple walnut shell and straw for a peasant.

Between 1600 and 1650 tobacco established itself as an important commodity. The booming market was supplied by the Spanish from the Caribbean and the British from their plantation colony in Virginia where the finest leaf, until supply increased to match demand, was reputed to be worth its weight in silver. The habit frequently took a firm hold before local authorities had developed a policy towards it, and customs regulations were hurriedly retrofitted to an already established trade. Many kingdoms and principalities enacted bans, including some of the

Opposite: Inns and taverns were rapidly colonized by the new smoking habit, which combined congenially with drinking, conversation and card games, as in this seventeenth-century Dutch scene.

Right: During the eighteenth century, snuff established itself in gentlemanly circles, allowing the elite to distinguish themselves from the common mass of pipe-smokers. Snuff-boxes became ornate and often costly accessories. This humorous example from the late eighteenth century depicts one gentleman being made sick by too much smoking, while the other considerately holds his wig.

Right: A New World tobacco plantation in the late seventeenth century: black workers pick, bundle, ferment and cure the leaves under the supervision of a European overseer. By this time plantation owners were replacing European indentured servants and convicts with African slave labour.

German states, where tobacco had spread quickly from the great entre-pots in Holland, and in Russia, where smokers ran the risk of being publicly flogged and having their noses slit. But prohibitions proved unpopular, expensive and impossible to enforce, and most states gravi-tated towards a system of licensed ports and traders or excise duties. By 1646, when the modernizing Peter the Great decided to replace Russia's ban with a tax, all the European powers had recognized that the policy of least resistance was also the policy of greatest profit.

Tobacco appeared in the Old World as part of an invasion of novel mood-altering imported 'soft drugs'. Coffee, cocoa and tea all converged on

Folio 305

Americain a'
Sa C...
latie...
et So...
Gobele...

Rameau de
L'árbre du Cacao

Cacao

Gousses de V...

Traité Nouveau, & Curieux du Chocolate
Composé Par Philippe Sylvestre Dufour

Right: The Spanish conquistadors found that the most highly esteemed drink among the Aztecs was chocolate, made from fermented cocoa seeds, which contain the stimulant theobromine. Moctezuma reportedly consumed nothing else, and cocoa beans were even used as currency by his people. Chocolate rapidly became a favourite luxury of the Spanish court, and colonists began cultivating the tree in the Caribbean, as depicted in Phillipe Sylvestre Dufour's *Traitez nouveaux et curieux du café, du thé et du chocolate*, published in Lyon in 1688.

Europe from east and west as global exploration opened up new trade routes. Like tobacco, all arrived with extravagant medical claims and counter-claims, alternately hailed as health-giving elixirs and condemned as pernicious and enervating luxuries. Each was subject to local or national bans before a regime of taxes and licences settled around them; and each was gradually adapted to suit the European market.

The European desire for these exotic novelties was not entirely unprecedented. The courts of medieval Europe had developed a passion for spices, which were believed to originate in Paradise itself. They were sold on the luxury market for huge profit and consumed in prodigious quantities; indeed, the discovery of the New World had been an accidental

byproduct of attempts to expand the spice trade. But the market for the new 'soft drugs' encompassed a far larger class of consumers, and appealed to the new ethic of individualism. The ideas of the Reformation were elaborating forms of private life where citizens expressed their personal preferences through consumption and by frequenting new forms of public space such as the coffee house. In a culture poor in native stimulants and euphoriants, the new drugs offered alternatives to alcohol that were more congenial to the values of sobriety, decency and productivity. They generated new forms of trade and profit, not merely in the drugs themselves, but in the cups, pipes, pots, jars, spoons and snuff boxes produced by manufactories across the continent in distinctive local styles.

Sauffen wir uns gleich zu tode
so geschichts doch nach der Mode.

Where tobacco was the universal accompaniment to the drugs of the New World, all these 'soft drugs' rose to popularity in conjunction with another new psychoactive substance or 'drug food': refined sugar. Originally produced in New Guinea and Indonesia, sugar had, like coffee, been patched into the global economy by the Arab trade network and had 'followed the Koran' to Spain, from where Columbus had introduced it to the Caribbean on his second voyage. Sugar plantations in British, French and Spanish colonies such as Jamaica and Santo Domingo, initially cleared and worked by natives and indentured convicts, had become massive enterprises driven by European capital and African slave labour, and the

Atlantic trade was now supplying it in industrial quantities to Europe, where it had previously been a rarity.

Like the other New World drugs, sugar arrived as a medicine. Its concentrated calories gave it miraculous powers of energy and nutrition for babies, invalids and the elderly, but it was not long before the wider population demonstrated the untapped potential of the European sweet tooth, which thus far had been limited to fruit and honey. The sugar buzz was addictive: doses that initially produced nausea quickly became tolerated, and produced cravings for more. It became a condiment, a medicine and a preservative; it was added to meat to make it richer, and to beer to make it stronger. In particular, it transformed the new soft drugs into more appealing forms. Amerindian cultures and palates had a predilection for concentrated, black and bitter liquids; in Europe, New World drugs were acculturated to local tastes by being sweetened, creamed and spiced. Tobacco ropes were cured with molasses; a cup of sugared tea or coffee was a calorie-rich substitute for a meal; sweetened chocolate bonbons and pastilles represented the height of luxury and

Below: African slaves working on a Caribbean sugar plantation, in an illustration from 1595. Over the next century, booming European demand would fuel an intensive system of mass production that demanded slave labour on an unprecedented scale.

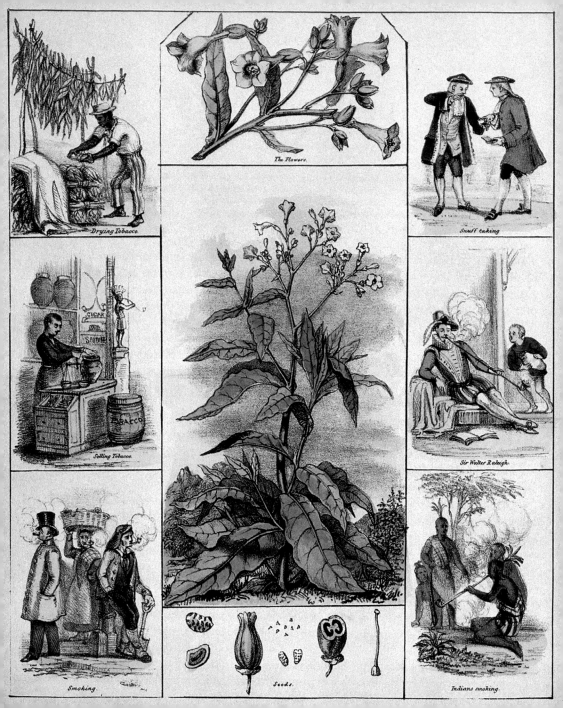

The Flowers.

Drying Tobacco.

Snuff taking.

Selling Tobacco.

Sir Walter Ralegh.

Smoking.

Seeds.

Indians smoking.

Right: Portuguese traders in India feasting in a bathing pool, in an Indian watercolour from 1540. The Portuguese introduced tobacco to the Indian nobility, who adopted it as a luxury commodity and traded it for textiles.

Below: Although the American plantations continued to dominate the global trade, by the eighteenth century, tobacco was being grown across the Old World from West Africa to Japan, and small-scale tobacco manufactories had emerged to supply local markets.

intoxicant' appealed to Chinese society just as it did to the new middling classes of Europe. It was first introduced in 1581 by the Jesuit missionary Matteo Ricci in the form of snuff, which quickly became an elite habit, mixed with other precious substances like musk and generating a fashion for ornate snuff boxes. By the early seventeenth century smoking had begun to take hold in the south, and by 1630 it was a common sight across swathes of the coast and interior, and in port cities such as Shanghai.

The Qing dynasty of Manchus who conquered China in 1644 had already adopted tobacco, but were alarmed at its growth among their new subjects, particularly their army, to whom they proclaimed that its use was 'a more heinous crime even than that of neglecting archery'. They imposed a prohibition on tobacco, but this was widely ignored, and smoking continued to penetrate the public and private worlds of soldiers and intellectuals, nobles and peasants, men, women and children. Variants on the European name were replaced with coinages such as 'smoke liquor' or, most commonly, chi yan, 'eating smoke'. In the absence of imperial approval it drew its sanction from medicine where, as in Europe, it was seen as 'hot' and 'dry', and a prophylactic against colds and malaria. Unlike in Europe, however, there was an existing medical culture to which tobacco smoking could be affixed: the practice of moxa, or the burning of herbs on the skin to draw out noxious humours and vapours in conditions such as rheumatism. Moxa was part of a broader medico-magical use of burning herbs and incenses to dispel unwanted influences, and tobacco benefited from the associations of smoke with purification, good luck and banishing bad spirits.

By 1700 tobacco was widespread across the entire Middle Kingdom, and the southern provinces of China were starting to adopt a new smoking mixture known as madak: tobacco mixed with a boiled solution of opium. Madak was produced by the Dutch empire in Java, where both plants were widely cultivated and traded; the Dutch had been supplying opium to China in modest quantities since the arrival of tobacco around 1630. The spread of madak was limited, but it coincided with a period of imperial instability and bureaucratic watchfulness, and provoked an edict in 1729 deploring the drug and its potential for tempting young men into smoking houses that might become hotbeds of subversive activity. The Yongzheng edict, as it was known, prohibited the importation of opium except for strictly medical uses.

But banning opium was no more effective than banning tobacco had been. By the end of the eighteenth century it was being imported in large quantities, mostly on Portuguese vessels; its price had dropped, and it was being smoked without tobacco in specially designed pipes, usually made of bamboo with silver decorations and clay bowls. These pipes

Following pages: Batavia, on the north-western tip of the island of Java, was the headquarters of the Dutch East India Company and the main entrepot for the trade in tobacco and opium across Asia. Its Town Hall still stands in the old quarter of present-day Jakarta.

Mandarin Civil

Right: A Chinese mandarin depicted with a long-stemmed opium pipe in an aquatint from around 1820. At this point most of the opium entering China was either grown by the Portuguese in Goa or imported from Bengal by Dutch traders.

reflected the fact that opium was different from tobacco: to release its intoxicating smoke, it needed to be not burnt but carefully vaporized. Small pellets of the drug, boiled with water into a treacly paste, were placed on the surface of the clay bowl with a pin, heated gently from the edges and consumed in a single inhalation. As a contraband substance, opium was not for sale in shops, but its reputation preceded it as it spread through well-established smuggler networks. The Shanghai poet Chen Cong's *Yancao Pu* ('Tobacco Manual') of 1805 describes opium intoxication as 'the realm of perfect happiness'.

Meanwhile, another drug had been making the opposite transit. Tea is native to the south-western regions of China; it had been used as a medicinal beverage for over a thousand years, and since at least the tenth century had been a staple of the Chinese and Japanese economies, with taxes to match. In 1610 the first tea shipment arrived in Europe, exported by Chinese junks to Java and then imported to Holland by the Dutch East

India Company. It joined the long list of coveted luxury products under Chinese monopoly control, recommended by European doctors as a cleansing tonic for liver and kidneys: the more the better, up to a hundred cups a day.

The tea habit remained an acquired and expensive taste in Europe until 1688, when the Glorious Revolution seated a Dutch monarch on the English throne. Thereafter, tea appeared more regularly and affordably in the nation's shops, and the British East India Company started to import it directly. It proved immensely popular in England, far more so than on the European mainland, supplanting coffee at breakfast, in the home, and even in London's thriving coffee houses. Britain's imports grew from

Right: A tea-drinker in nineteenth-century Taiwan. The Chinese use of tea (*cha*) as a medicine and an aid to wakefulness dates back to the first millennium BC. It was established as a social and ceremonial beverage by the early years of the Tang Dynasty, around 700 AD.

200 pounds a year in 1688 to over a million by 1721, and over four million by 1750. For the East India Company who held a monopoly on the trade, and for the government who taxed it to the hilt, the national obsession was hugely profitable. Yet demand still outstripped supply, and smuggled tea invaded the market, often adulterated with local leaves – typically sloe for green tea, and hawthorn for black – and with its tannin colours approximated by toxic chemicals including Prussian blue and verdigris. By 1784 there was almost as much counterfeit tea in Britain as genuine leaf, and customs fleets were at full stretch attempting to stem the smuggling trade along the south coast. The government was forced to slash taxes from their profiteering level of 119% to a modest 12% to regain control of the market.

SOWING THE TEA

Opposite and below: Tea produced in China for export was planted in rows (*opposite*), and the young leaves picked, graded and trimmed to remove the dead sections. The selected leaves were rolled into balls and dried in ovens before being packed into canisters and transported, often on rafts (*below*), to the ports where foreigners were permitted to trade.

The British addiction to tea was now making healthy profits for importers and merchants, but it was having a ruinous effect on the national treasury. One reason for the high government taxes was that the East India Company was obliged to pay its Chinese suppliers for tea in silver, as it had few commodities for which the Chinese were interested in trading, now that tobacco was widely grown in provinces such as Yunnan. Between 1800 and 1810, nearly a thousand tons of British silver haemorrhaged to the Chinese treasury. It was against this background that the East India Company began to take an interest in the booming market for opium around the south China coast, where a thoroughly international assortment of traders and pirates – Dutch, Armenian, Persian, Danish,

TEA SENT OFF AS PACKED.

American, Portuguese and British – were by now supplying the illicit market. Furthermore, they were trading it directly for silver bullion.

The East India Company were well placed to ply this shady but lucrative trade. Opium had been grown in the west of India by the Portuguese in the sixteenth century and the Dutch in the seventeenth, but the richest plantations were in the east, across the Ganges plains from Bengal to Benares, and these had fallen into British hands with the collapse of the Mughal empire. Opium growing was labour intensive, and the disruption and displacement had left many of the plantations neglected or abandoned. The Company reorganized them into an efficient agribusiness, with a system of advance payment to farmers for every stage of the process – seeding, planting, harvesting, harrowing – to keep the fields fertile and productive. The opium was stored in huge factories at Patna, the traditional centre of the opium-growing region, and sold by private auction at Calcutta.

The British attitude to opium was ambivalent from the start. Warren Hastings, the first Governor General of Bengal, had regarded it as a 'pernicious item of luxury', the sale of which needed to be placed under some form of official control. If every merchant and nation was allowed to buy opium, the bidding war would raise prices and increase production,

Opposite: European traders discuss terms with a Chinese merchant (*opposite above*) while the tea is transferred from wicker canisters to wooden packing crates in preparation for its voyage. This business was conducted in 'factories', such as the one at Canton (*opposite below*) where foreigners were permitted to reside and trade under their national flags.

Right and following pages: Opium production on an industrial scale in Patna, India. The resin is mixed in troughs (*right*) until it is the right consistency for forming into balls, which are stacked in a huge warehouse complex (*following pages*).

flooding the world with a potent and dangerous drug at prices that would encourage its misuse. On the other hand, prohibiting the trade would only gift it to the illicit contraband market, as was already the case in China, and there was little appetite in Britain for suppressing such a profitable crop. It was decided that the best solution was for the trade to become a Company monopoly. With British government approval, Dutch stocks of Indian opium were bought up and the East India Company cornered the market in the one commodity that the Chinese valued more than silver.

There was, however, a serious obstacle to the trade: the Chinese prohibition. By 1820 the business was, although illegal, relatively formalized. Smuggling vessels, usually fast clippers, would head for the mouth of the Pearl River below the port of Canton. They would pass the Portuguese trade enclave of Macao and put in at Lintin Island, a jagged mountain outcrop in the Canton bay. Here, fifty-oared Chinese boats, known as 'centipedes' or 'scrambling dragons', would dash out to meet them, exchange chests of opium for previously negotiated quantities of silver and then beach the opium at hidden spots along the coast. Although the trade was carried out in sight of the Emperor's harbour-masters and customs officers, who were cut in on the deal, it could only be transacted by pirates who had nothing to lose. If the East India Company attempted the same, it would not only be condemned by British public opinion but would run the risk of losing the tea concession that was its lifeblood.

The obvious solution to this problem was to sell through intermediaries, which became considerably easier after the Company's trade monopoly with China was brought to an end in 1831. Now the British government could work hand-in-glove with independent British operators, while still maintaining a public façade of separation from the business. The most ambitious and well-known of these smugglers was the firm of Jardine and Matheson, a pair of Scottish entrepreneurs who had previously traded in Dutch opium and built up a fleet of the fastest clippers in the world, known as 'greyhounds of the seas'. In the East, they were discreet about their role in the opium trade, justifying their presence on the south China coast as missionary activity distributing bibles; back in Britain, they were well-connected political lobbyists, arguing for the principle of free trade and against the illegitimate imperial ban on the desires of the people. Industrial production of opium in Bengal was now matched by the world's most efficient shipping system, and by 1840 Jardine and Matheson were selling six thousand opium chests a year. Over the decade between 1830 and 1840 the British trade deficit was reversed, and the treasury received a surplus of 366 tons of Chinese silver.

Opposite: Opium has been cultivated in India since antiquity; it is said to have been introduced by Alexander the Great. It was commonly eaten or drunk, as it continues to be in areas such as Rajasthan today. Here, in a painting made around 1810, ascetics in Udaipur prepare and consume opium as part of their devotions .

With China struggling against floods, famines and an economic
depression, and the imperial court consumed by conflicts and rebellions,
British traders became more brazen in flouting the opium prohibition,
and even attempted to discuss the business with high officials behind the
Emperor's back. This was an insult that could not go unpunished, and in
1839 the Emperor appointed a new commissioner, Lin Zexu, a highly
capable and scrupulous minister with orders to root out official corruption, dismantle all informal arrangements with opium smugglers and
crack down hard on the illegal trade. When the British traders ignored his
orders, Lin imprisoned them in their offices until they surrendered their
stocks: 2,613,879 lbs of opium, the best part of a year's supply. He considered burning it, but feared that the residue would still be smokable, so on
17 June 1839 he had it thrown into the harbour and churned with salt and
lime to prevent it being recovered. When he followed this insult with an
admonition to Queen Victoria to destroy all opium within her territories,
the British parliament declared war and dispatched a fleet of gunships
that sailed up the estuary and pounded the harbour of Chusan to rubble.

After further raids along the coast, in 1842 the Chinese signed the
Treaty of Nanking, legitimizing the opium trade and ceding the island of
Hong Kong to Britain. Skirmishes resumed in a second war of 1856–60,
in which British troops advanced as far as Beijing and destroyed the
Emperor's Summer Palace. With the Opium Wars, as the conflicts
became known, they destroyed China's pretensions to imperial status
and reduced her to the level of a semi-colony: a warehouse of foreign
goods, traded across the global market on British terms. By monopolizing

On the other side of the world, however, China's relationship with opium was viewed very differently. To the Christian missionaries who were the main source of reportage, the nation was in the grip of mass addiction to the 'opium scourge'. Plantations took over arable land while peasants starved; opium shops and houses in every town sapped the national economy; in areas of famine, sallow and emaciated smokers by the roadsides were visibly reducing themselves to a living death. These reports rekindled the political debate that had preceded the Opium Wars: though the foreign secretary, Lord Palmerston, had comfortably won the vote for war on the grounds of China's destruction of British property, the young William Gladstone had pronounced the opium business a

THE QUEEN OF CHINATOWN

BY JOSEPH JARROW

HURLED BY HIGHBINDERS THROUGH THE RAT PIT'S DOUBLE TRAP.

'permanent disgrace' to the nation, and the Earl of Shaftesbury had called the 'nefarious traffic' worse than the slave trade. This had long been the view of religious groups such as the Quakers, and had subsequently gained much ground in progressive, reform-minded civil society. In 1874 this opposition was focused by the formation of the Anglo-Oriental Society for the Suppression of the Opium Trade, a coalition of Quakers and missionaries campaigning to force Britain out of the Chinese opium market, who painted a devastating picture of a nation enslaved by the 'opium evil'. As the anti-opium campaign laid claim to the moral high ground, it became influential enough for notorious traders such as Jardine and Matheson to withdraw from the business (which had in any case become less profitable as the Chinese home-grown crop increased).

Although opium was a familiar medicine in the West, the idea of smoking it for pleasure was novel and shocking. Like the fate of the Native American when exposed to alcohol, it suggested that certain drugs might be manageable in one culture but terminally destructive in another. Medical opinion was split. In the letters column of The Times, doctors who called it a 'demoralizing vice' were answered by others who insisted it was 'harmless and beneficial', but the profession was already abandoning opium tinctures in favour of pure drugs, such as morphine, administered by specialists.

As well as ethical and medical concerns, the anti-opium campaign drew on a growing fear of the Chinese communities in the ports, slums and Chinatowns of the West. As the nineteenth century drew to its close, images of 'Oriental contagion' crowded upon one another and became a staple of mass popular culture. It was the opening of Charles Dickens's Edwin Drood, serialized in 1870, that first introduced to British readers the vision of the opium den concealed in the grim tenements of Limehouse and Poplar, around London's docks: stinking alleys, crowded hovels and lice-infested bunks with British, Chinese and Lascar sailors huddled together while an old hag, who has over long years of debauchery 'smoked herself into a strange likeness of the Chinaman', tends the pipe and smears opium dross across its bowl with a filthy brooch-pin.

Dickens's account was worked up from a visit to the home of Ah Sing, a Chinese gentleman who had arrived in London's East End in the 1860s and was a familiar local curiosity: he had even been visited by the Prince of Wales. It was luridly illustrated by Gustave Doré, and elaborated across hundreds of fictional and faux-documentary accounts by popular writers from Oscar Wilde to Arthur Conan Doyle. Through these nightmarish scenes, the opium den became a terminus of the damned: the free-falling West End roué committing slow suicide a world away from his gambling debts and extra-marital scandals or, increasingly, the chorus

Opposite: The 'Yellow Peril': opium dens, and particularly the spectacle of vulnerable white women enslaved by the drug, became a staple ingredient in sensational and villainous portrayals of Chinatown, as in this poster for a Broadway melodrama of 1899.

Above and right: The image of the opium den in Victorian London drew heavily on the home of Ah Sing in the dockland area of Limehouse, which Charles Dickens visited before writing *Edwin Drood*. It was portrayed in sinister chiaroscuro by Gustave Doré (*above*) in his *London: A Pilgrimage* (1872); this oil painting by an unknown artist (*right*) depicts one of Ah Sing's visitors, probably a Chinese sailor.

operating over 1,500 opium dens across Vietnam, Laos and Cambodia. By this point ex-colonials and merchant sailors returning to France had set up similar establishments (*opposite*), particularly in ports such as Marseilles and Toulon.

Opposite: The French

Dix-Neuvième année. — N° 941. Huit pages : CINQ centimes Dimanche 17 Février 1907.

Le Petit Parisien

SUPPLÉMENT LITTÉRAIRE ILLUSTRÉ

TOUS LES JOURS
Le Petit Parisien
(Six pages)
5 centimes

CHAQUE SEMAINE
LE SUPPLÉMENT LITTÉRAIRE
5 centimes

DIRECTION: 18, rue d'Enghien (10ᵉ), PARIS

ABONNEMENTS
PARIS ET DÉPARTEMENTS:
12 mois, 4 fr. 50. 6 mois, 2 fr. 25
UNION POSTALE:
12 mois, 5 fr. 50. 6 mois, 3 fr.

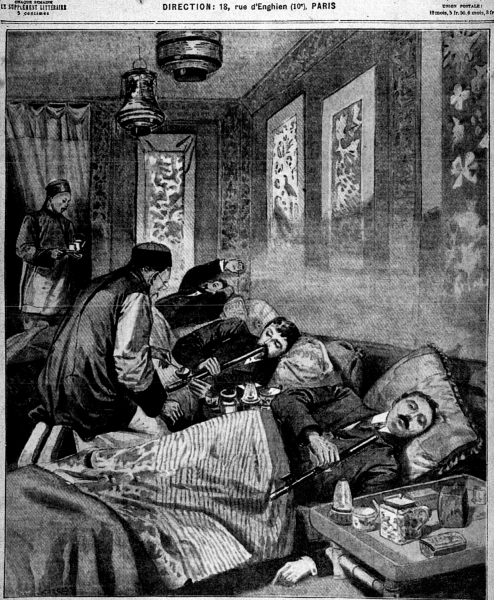

UNE FUMERIE D'OPIUM EN FRANCE

girl lured into prostitution and slavery by the Chinese underworld kingpin, a character who found his fictional apotheosis in 1913 in Sax Rohmer's *The Mystery of Fu Manchu*, 'the yellow peril incarnate in one man'.

It was in this climate of fear, and with emigration booming as Chinese workers sought to escape poverty at home, that the first prohibitions of opium were introduced. In San Francisco, where railway-building 'coolies' formed the largest Chinese population in the Western world, the Opium Exclusion Act of 1875 criminalized the smoking of opium by Chinese (but not by whites) after a public campaign that focused on the dangers of racial mixing, and particularly the threat to vulnerable white women. In 1887 America banned the import of Chinese opium and, as it made its belated entry into the colonial era, it exported similar prohibitions abroad. In the Philippines, annexed during the Spanish–American War in 1898, the Chinese opium trade was banned, and the drug restricted to medical use by the Philippino population. A lobby of religious voices began to press for an American-led effort to control the opium traffic by international treaty; they coalesced around the Episcopalian bishop Charles Brent, whose service on the Philippines opium commission had convinced him that 'unwholesome pleasure-seeking' and the 'crude temptations of the Orient' were corrupting both Asians and their American occupiers.

The initiative took on the dimension of a moral crusade, and was highly effective in exposing the ignoble motives of those who resisted. In 1895 Britain appointed a Royal Commission to examine the opium question. It concluded that a ban would be an unjust imposition of colonial authority on native interests; several Indian witnesses had argued that it would make more sense to ban alcohol to the British. But the report was easily characterized as a whitewash influenced by British trade interests, and other opium-trading nations, such as Portugal, France and Persia, were forced into justifications of the trade that sounded as specious as those of Britain half a century before. In 1909 an International Opium Commission, convened in Shanghai, agreed the resolution that opiates were a 'grave danger' demanding international regulation; the first International Conference on Opium, convened at the Hague in 1911 and chaired by Bishop Brent, obliged its signatories to enact strict domestic legislation in preparation for a binding international treaty. America, newly arrived on the world stage, was taking the lead in redressing the unacceptable face of colonialism.

The Republic of China, as it had recently become, was an enthusiastic participant in the crusade. The Boxer Rebellion of 1900 had been driven by popular revulsion against the old imperial culture: pigtails were replaced with short hair, robes with work shirts and trousers, and opium

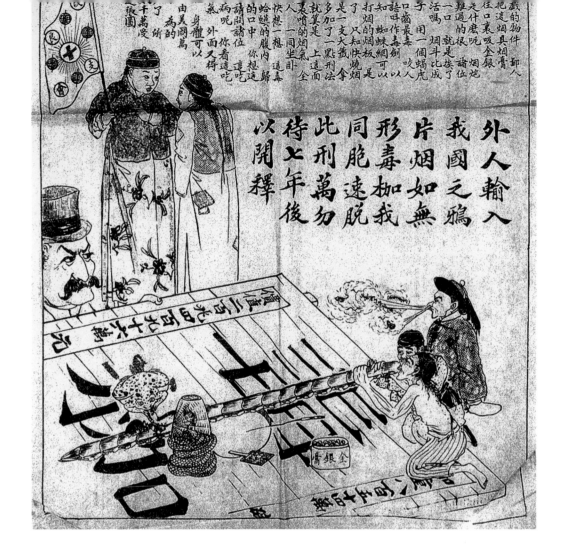

Above: An early Chinese anti-opium poster from 1863. A toad clings to the opium pipe, the exhaled smoke is full of centipedes and the characters underneath the pipe read 'poison yoke'.

with cigarettes. The drug habit of the previous generation became the favourite symbol of China's humiliation by the West: 'foreign mud' that had been peddled by pirates and evil empires to sap their economy and reduce their population to misery. Recalcitrant opium users were forced into detoxification clinics and asylums run by missionary groups, where they were subject to various 'opium cures', among them the current Western trend for substituting opium with other drugs including strychnine, quinine, caffeine and particularly morphine or heroin, usually by hypodermic injection.

But the cure turned out to be worse than the disease. Just as the smoking habit had a fortuitous resemblance to native practices such as incense and *moxa*, the hypodermic resonated with the long-established traditions of acupuncture. Whereas Westerners found the needle shocking, in China it became an eagerly sought-after status symbol. Opium houses in the coastal cities were replaced by inns and gambling dens where shots of the 'magic needle' cost less than a smoke, but claimed a far higher price in addictions, and introduced previously unknown health problems. Needles, rarely cleaned between injections, spread blood-borne diseases, and men with bodies covered in sores and abscesses became a common sight in the dens of Shanghai.

Compared to the situation in China, the suppression of opium was of minor consequence in Europe and America, where many of its medical virtues were now available from synthetic substitutes ranging from aspirin to chloral hydrate. In the West, the most serious problem was not opium but alcohol. From 1880 to 1920, the 'alcohol question' would become the focal issue for a transformative social movement – and, in America in particular, a defining fault-line across the landscape of politics.

As the medical professions grew in stature throughout the nineteenth century, and public health initiatives such as sanitation and immunization brought their influence and authority into the affairs of state, it became ever more obvious that excessive use of alcohol, especially strong spirits, was an exacerbating factor in many social ills: poverty, unemployment, crime and epidemic disease. Alcohol itself could not be blamed, since it was prevalent across all sectors of society, not least among politicians and legislators. Medical theories began to place more weight on ideas of problematic 'types' with psychological weaknesses, typically members of the social and economic underclass. The term 'alcoholic' came into common use, alongside coinages such as 'addict' and 'narcomaniac', to classify anyone with an underlying pathology that made alcohol and other drugs not a recreation but a medical problem.

The emerging medical orthodoxy was in tune with established religious opinion that held drunkenness to be a sin, and sobriety to bring an individual closer to God, but it resonated equally with progressive and liberal opinions. Temperance became a central cause in the women's movement, which saw alcohol as the agent of a vicious circle of poverty and misery. It encouraged working men to spend their wages in taverns outside the factory gate rather than passing them on to their wives for the household budget; it abetted domestic violence and poverty, and impeded savings, education and social progress. As Temperance societies took their mission into the slums and factory towns of Europe and America, urging the working classes to 'take the pledge', public opinion came to reflect their conviction that the nineteenth century's tolerance of the evils of alcohol could have no place in the civilized society of the twentieth.

Right and below: Temperance campaigns made frequent use of shock imagery. In *The Drunkard's Progress* (right), an American hand-coloured lithograph from 1846, 'a glass with a friend' leads to 'death by suicide'; in *The Drunkard's Children* (below), a George Cruikshank etching published in London in 1848, the destitute family is abandoned to the gin shop and its criminal milieu.

Above and opposite: The benefits of temperance were seen as extending beyond physical health to improve an individual's moral character and social standing (*opposite*). Temperance events were often grand social affairs, such as this banquet in Cork, Ireland, in 1843 (*above*).

In Europe, the Temperance movement cut across political allegiances, but in America it became the lightning-rod for a fierce culture war that would make it the most divisive political issue since slavery. In thousands of small towns throughout the country social rifts were opening between an 'uptown' that reflected the established Anglo-Saxon culture, typically centred on Sunday attendance at the church, and a 'downtown' community of more recent immigrant groups – Italian, Irish, German – whose most visible expression was the crowded tavern on Saturday night. As these recent arrivals became more prosperous, not least through the brewery business, they came to challenge the political dominance of the town and city founders. The 'dry' platform of alcohol prohibition became a powerful shorthand for opposition to 'wet' candidates, who were cast as the protectors of brewery interests and other corrupt business practices.

It was highly advantageous for the traditionalists to frame their cultural struggle around the 'alcohol question'. To argue for the benefits of intoxication was to defend the indefensible: as with tobacco today, its only organized defenders were the alcohol industry itself and their vested interests. The argument against intoxication with other drugs was carried almost invisibly in its wake: there were no public defenders for a

THE TREE OF TEMPERANCE.

PUBLISHED BY CURRIER & IVES   Entered, according to act of Congress in the year 1872, by Currier & Ives, in the Office of the Librarian of Congress at Washington.   125 NASSAU ST NEW YORK.

Ye shall know them by their fruits. Do men gather grapes of thorns, or figs of thistles? Matt. VII. 16   Ho, every one that thirsteth, come ye to the waters, Isaiah LV.17. And be not drunk with wine, wherein is excess, Ephesians V 18   And if he thirsts give him water to drink, Prov.XXV. And he shall be like a tree planted by the rivers of water, that bringeth forth fruit in his season, his leaf also shall not wither & whatsoever he doeth shall prosper, Psalms 1. 3

population of drug consumers composed mostly of ethnic minorities, medical patients and a small subculture of bohemians and petty criminals. The public debate shifted from whether intoxication was a problem to how the problem should be conceived and addressed. 'Is it', asked Norman Kerr, the British doctor who founded the Society for the Study of Inebriety, 'a sin, a crime, a vice or a disease?'. Depending on the answer to this question, the solution might be higher taxation, public education, state monopoly, medical controls or outright criminalization.

All these options were deployed, in different nations and in different combinations. In 1905 Sweden became the first country to enforce a state

Above: The monster of alcohol is attacked by a woman with a mallet in this Dutch poster from 1928.

Right: In France, the evils of alcohol were particularly associated with absinthe, a potent distilled spirit infused with fennel and wormwood, as featured in this poster from 1910.

monopoly on alcohol production and sale; in Britain and other European nations, the First World War expedited the introduction of licensing laws that specified standard drink measures and limited the hours in which alcohol could be sold. Public information campaigns were vigorously promoted by civil and medical groups, along with medical treatments for alcoholism. In 1915 alcohol was prohibited in Iceland, and in 1916 in Norway. In America, the same coalition that had driven the prohibition of opium into international law now mobilized for the national prohibition of all alcoholic beverages. Moderates argued that beer and wine were relatively harmless, and the ban should be confined to spirits, but the 'dry' lobby pushed their advantage to the full, and on 28 October 1919 the Volstead Act brought in an eighteenth amendment to the US Constitution that prohibited the manufacture, import or sale of intoxicating liquors.

Below: An iconic image of the Prohibition Era: casks of illegal alcohol being poured into the New York City sewers. Enforcement successes were photographed and widely publicized, even as a huge illicit market was maintained by pervasive police corruption.

The 'noble experiment', however, did not deliver the expected results. Within weeks the Prohibition Era had become the Roaring Twenties, with the alcohol trade enthusiastically taken over by organized crime. Prices tripled and, with taxes and quality control non-existent, there was plenty of profit available to bribe and co-opt police and judiciaries. Big cities such as Chicago swiftly fell under the control of crime syndicates beyond

the reach of the law. Deaths from alcohol rose as the economics of prohibition supplied it in its most concentrated and potent forms; beer was mostly replaced by the more lucrative whisky and rye, often contaminated with denatured methanol. But most significantly, the law lacked public support. Alcohol was too widespread across society, and the extent of its dangers too well understood, for its cultural sanction to be withdrawn simply by act of Congress. Before Prohibition, 'big government' had been perceived as being hand-in-glove with the alcohol industry; now politicians, many of whom were private drinkers, were seen as posturing hypocrites, no better than the gangsters who were increasingly portrayed as popular heroes. Drinking spread into classes of society where it had not established itself before, notably among young women, for whom the cocktail was invented as a palatable vehicle for the ubiquitous strong spirits.

When alcohol prohibition was repealed in 1932, one of the side effects was to intensify the prohibition of other drugs. Thousands of police and administrators from the Alcohol Bureau, facing an uncertain future in the Depression, migrated to the Narcotics Bureau whose chief, Harry Anslinger, campaigned vigorously to prioritize the 'drug menace'. He expanded the category to include cannabis, which he rechristened 'marijuana' to stress its connection with the Mexican immigrant community, distinguishing it from the familiar and innocuous-sounding 'hemp' and tapping into Depression-era racial anxieties. The Narcotics Bureau spearheaded American efforts to expand the international drug laws, and global prohibition was eventually codified in 1961 by the United Nations Single Convention on Narcotic Drugs, which obliged every UN member to enshrine the prohibition of opiates, coca products and cannabis in their domestic policy.

Ironically, this was precisely the point at which the global prohibition of drugs began to fail. Until the 1960s, trade and supply controls had largely succeeded in confining demand to the localized subcultures of the previous century: cannabis use remained widespread in India without establishing itself in the West, and heroin circulated in criminal subcultures without spreading to the wider population. But now the world's markets were opening up as never before, and a curious, individualistic and prosperous younger generation, the first to be raised as truly global consumers, awakened to the realization that alcohol was not the world's only intoxicant. An international counterculture spread the news of hashish-smoking in Morocco and LSD discovered in Swiss laboratories, the benzedrine pills that propelled truck drivers through the night and the hallucinogenic mushrooms consumed in remote Mexican villages. Suddenly humanity's knowledge of mind-altering drugs, assembled

Right: Until 1900 the cannabis plant was widely cultivated in America and known by its traditional name, hemp. By adopting the foreign term 'marijuana' (sometimes spelled 'marihuana') in the 1930s, anti-drug campaigns created a new set of associations – immigrant underworlds, vice and narcotic addiction – exploited for maximum sensational effect in this movie poster from the period.

through centuries and across continents, was being collected into an illicit global formulary, refined and expanded by a cult of enthusiastic self-experimentation.

This was a situation for which the international drug laws had not been designed, and which they were powerless to contain. Prohibition had been effective at nipping demand in the bud, but once an international market was firmly established, its effects became perverse and counterproductive. Growing demand increased profit margins, drawing more criminal interests into the trade. Anti-trafficking operations, where they succeeded, only drove prices up further and created new supply routes elsewhere. Just as during alcohol prohibition, the economics of

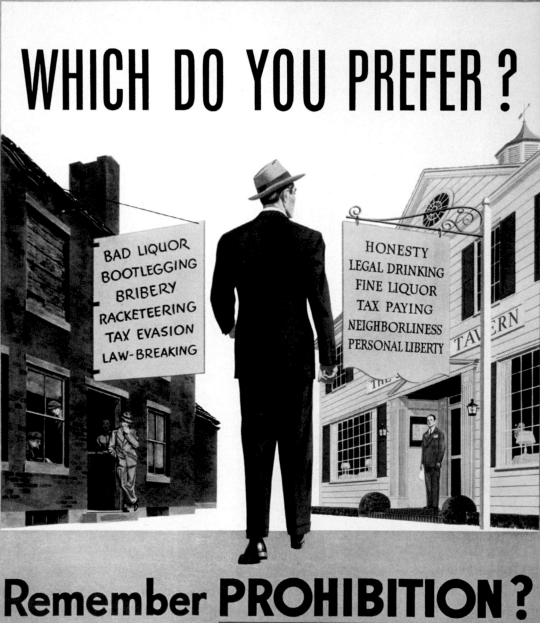

supply tended to concentrate the product into its most lucrative and dangerous form: morphine became heroin, cocaine became crack, cannabis became skunk. Cultural currents carried demand around the globe, and criminal cartels cycled their profits with impunity through an ever-shifting network of kleptocracies, tax havens and failed states.

This endgame has been reached many times before: not just with the collapse of alcohol prohibition in America, but ever since the European tobacco prohibitions at the dawn of the global drug trade. Demand, once established, has a long history of outgunning even the most high-handed authorities. The drug habit is a cultural construct: official decrees may mitigate it, but their power to reverse its tide is limited. The 'war on drugs', as President Nixon christened it in 1971, was intended to turn back the clock to the previous era; but the consensus that it sought to impose was already a thing of the past. To succeed, it needed to convince the world that drugs were a genuine threat to civilization, and that there was a genuine hope of returning to a world without them. But such propositions become harder to sell with time, as emergency powers shade into autocracy and corruption, and cultural panic dissolves into business as usual.

Tobacco and sugar, having spread from America to Europe, have now conquered all but the most remote corners of the globe. They were followed by opium, travelling from Europe to Turkey to India to China and beyond. Cannabis radiated out from India into Africa and Europe, then via both channels to Brazil and the Americas. Cocaine spread from South to North America and Europe, and is now endemic in the cities of Asia and Africa. Opium, refined into heroin, has funded warlords and insurgencies from the Golden Triangle to Colombia to Afghanistan. The synthetic drugs of the twentieth century, from LSD to ecstasy to methamphetamine, are at home in an internationalized youth culture that spans Rio and Toronto, Helsinki and Sydney, Bangkok and Madrid, and the new drugs of the twenty-first century – ketamine, salvia, mephedrone – have achieved instant global fame and distribution via the internet. Over the last three centuries, this process of confluence and diffusion has determined the fate of empires and defined international trade. Today's illicit drugs trade, estimated by the UN at $350 billion USD a year, now constitutes one of the three largest international markets on the planet, along with arms and oil. Whether it remains prohibited, or is regulated and taxed, it will continue to drive the global economy of the future.

Yet drug use is not inevitably destined to escalate forever. Just as cultures begin their drug habits without official permission, they can equally curtail them at their own initiative. Perhaps the most conspicuous example

in the present day is tobacco: the very substance that, along with sugar, started the global drug trade. For four centuries, it has seduced the modern world via pipes and snuff, cigars and cigarettes, but in Europe and North America, where its global conquest began, the taste for it seems to be in decline. Tobacco has always been a social drug, an adjunct to meeting strangers, relaxing after work and sparking up conversations, a small gift that buys five minutes of informality and interaction, but now it is more commonly regarded as antisocial than convivial. During the Second World War, General Pershing famously declared that cigarettes were more important than food for troop morale; today, their packs are emblazoned with hideous images of emphysemic lungs. Throughout modernity, smokers have been the life and soul of the party; now they shiver on the street outside the office building, addicts isolated by their need for a fix.

This is, however, only the case for the Western minority. The global tobacco habit is far from being extinguished: in many parts of the developing world it is still spreading and the cultural attitude towards smoking remains very different. China, for example, where the cigarette first established itself as a modern substitute for the opium habit, is home to nearly a third of the world's smokers, some 300 million; here it remains a symbol of wealth, conviviality and sophistication. An international brand marks a businessman out as a cosmopolitan 'player'; an avant-garde artist poses with a cheap local smoke. In Japan, which has maintained a proudly distinctive smoking culture since it developed its own *kiseru* style of tobacco around 1700, cigarettes are produced and advertised by the government-controlled Japan Tobacco corporation. Official government policy discourages non-smokers and the young from starting, but the firm's statement of corporate responsibility includes 'respect for local norms and cultures', and insists 'we do not believe that there is a single, global "solution" to the tobacco controversy'.

The change in Western attitudes, though supported by governments and public health initiatives, is driven by the dawning realization that the risks of smoking, for those who would otherwise expect to live long and healthy lives, are on a scale that dwarfs any other mainstream form of consumption or leisure activity. Half of all lifetime users will die of their habit, meaning that it will kill half a billion people alive today. The demonstration of the link between smoking and lung cancer, made by Richard Doll in 1950, is potentially the most significant in the entire history of epidemiology, but it has registered more profoundly in some cultures than in others. In the modern West, its effect has been more pronounced among those of higher classes and incomes, and the drive to quit smoking has taken on the aspirational cast of the nineteenth-century

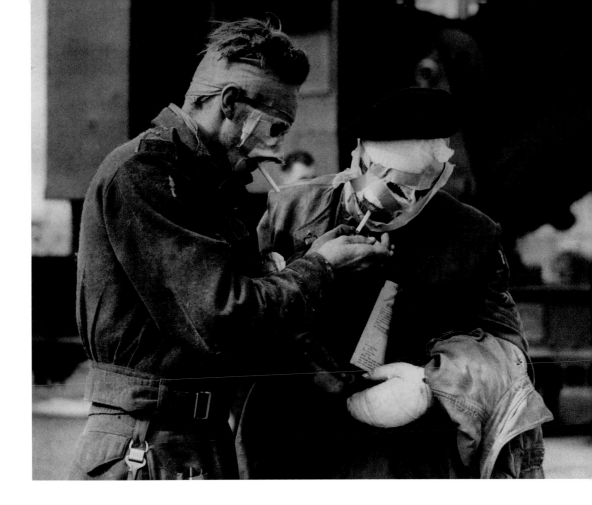

Temperance campaigns against alcohol. The Western world has not abandoned the habit *en masse* – in absolute terms, the decline in the number of smokers has been modest – but the social status of smoking has moved sharply downmarket.

An important component of this change in social attitudes has been the redefinition of the smoking habit as an addiction to nicotine. Drinking coffee is not conceived as caffeine addiction, but tobacco is now seen as a 'drug' in the pejorative sense of the term, and its users pathologized as addicts; indeed, many smokers now prefer to justify their habit as an addiction rather than as a personal choice or a moral weakness. But the relation of nicotine to the dangers of smoking is a curious one. Although it is powerfully toxic in larger doses – the amount of nicotine in a packet of cigarettes, if eaten, would be lethal – the drug as smoked is not particularly harmful; it is the tars in tobacco that deliver both the taste and the carcinogens. This means that the drug can be its own remedy: nicotine patches and gums have become a hugely profitable industry, a puritan substitution that turns poison into medicine by removing the element of pleasure. Nicotine is a useful stimulant, and the fact that it is harmless enough to be supplied pharmaceutically suggests that it may become popular in the future in a smoke-free form.

Although the new cultural attitudes to smoking are widely perceived as resulting from government controls and regulations, they are a broader response to the epidemiological evidence: the pressure to regulate emerged from public health and citizens' groups long before any official diktats. From the seventeenth century onwards, national governments have almost universally adopted the strategy of raising as much tax revenue from tobacco as the market will bear, and it is now clear that, particularly in the United States, administrations and tobacco lobbies colluded for decades in obfuscating public health evidence in the interest of protecting their revenue streams. In the decline of smoking, governments and nation-states are the losers. Tobacco duties raise vast sums, are easy to extract and politically hard to oppose, even though they fall disproportionately on the poor, and although smokers place a considerable burden on health services, they also relieve them by dying sooner. The most significant political initiatives have taken place on the international stage, particularly through the World Health Organization, whose Framework Convention on Tobacco Control, which came into force in 2005, defines tobacco purely as a health problem – 'the tobacco epidemic is a communicated disease' – and mandates that nation-states reduce demand by regulating products, advertising, sales to minors and smoke-free zones.

Yet if tobacco was nothing but a vector of disease and death, it could not have entwined itself into modernity as tightly as it did. Like all drugs, it offers benefits and extracts costs, in a ratio that varies between individuals and across cultures, and which is constantly adjusted over time. The ratio is markedly more positive in some substances than in others, but it can never be reduced to a definitive medical calculation: it is also determined by the forms and doses in which the drug is consumed, whether its trade is responsibly regulated or controlled by profiteers or criminals, and the ever-changing cultural spheres in which its use unfolds.

Tobacco has been called the shaman's curse on the West, his revenge for the inequalities of the Columbian exchange: the most prized of his sacred plants turned out to be a poison chalice. But to the Native Americans, tobacco's benefits were indeed great and its costs low, since most did not consume it at the levels of the habitual cigarette smoker, or live long enough to suffer its fatal consequences. For many across the developing world, the situation remains much the same today. It is in the wealthy enclaves of the West that the cost–benefit ratio has shifted most significantly, though even here its health harms are less of a deterrent to

Above: The World Health Organization campaigns for pictorial health warnings on cigarette packs.

Right: A young girl smokes a cigarette in Laos in 2008.

the young; only with increasing age do medical concerns begin to outweigh the social pleasures of smoking. Broadly speaking, the decline of tobacco seems to correlate with higher levels of wellbeing, education and the prospect of living a long and happy life. If so, the Age of Tobacco may be waning as science tips the scales decisively against it, but its twilight could still be a long one.

Notes and Further Reading

Chapter 1: A Universal Impulse

The Evolution of Drugs

Donald E. Brown's *Human Universals* (1981) has been widely referenced; his list of universals is discussed and reproduced in Steven Pinker's *The Blank Slate* (2003). There are some cultures (the most typically cited are Inuit groups) who have no intoxicating plants among their indigenous flora, but use techniques such as fasting and sleep deprivation to alter consciousness, and adopt foreign drugs such as alcohol and tobacco when they become available.

Gustav Schenk's *The Book of Poisons* (1956) remains an accessible introduction to the spectrum of plant poisons and intoxicants. Studies in the coevolution of plants and animals were pioneered by Paul Ehrlich and Peter Raven in their paper 'Butterflies and Plants: A study in coevolution', *Evolution* 18 (1964), pp. 586–608. The theory that plant drugs (specifically mushrooms) were the original spur to human brain development and language is advanced by Terence McKenna in *Food of the Gods* (1992).

Animal Intoxication

The development of psychoactive alkaloids is discussed in Ronald Siegel's *Intoxication: Life in pursuit of artificial paradise* (1989), a rich repository of information on drug experiments on animals. Additional zoological observations are reported in Giorgio Samorini's *Animals and Psychedelics* (2000).

The Rat Park experiments were published as B. K. Alexander, B. L. Beyerstein, P. F. Hadaway and R. B. Coambs, 'The effect of early and later colony housing on morphine ingestion in rats', *Pharmacology, Biochemistry and Behaviour* 15 (1981), pp. 571–76. The experiments are widely discussed, for example in Lauren Slater's *Opening Skinner's Box* (2004). Bruce Alexander expands the conclusions of Rat Park in The *Globalisation of Addiction* (2008).

Drugs and Shamanism

On the prehistory, history and ethnography of DMT-containing snuffs in South America, see Constantino Manuel Torres and David B. Repke, *Anadenanthera: Visionary plant of ancient South America* (2006).

Oriental Pipes, a nineteenth-century lithograph by Schmidt in Auguste Racinet's *Le Costume Historique*.

European archaeology presents a very different picture: intoxicating plants such as dried poppy capsules are found at burial sites dating back to 4000 BC, but there are no unambiguous drug artefacts or utensils present until a much later date. The origins of Old World drug use are discussed by Richard Rudgley in *The Alchemy of Culture* (1993), *Lost Civilisations of the Stone Age* (1998) and elsewhere. The earliest plausible European drug artefacts are Middle Neolithic pottery rings usually identified as 'vase supports', which Andrew Sherratt proposed as braziers for opium-smoke inhalation in his paper 'Sacred and Profane Substances: The ritual use of narcotics in late Neolithic Europe', in *Sacred and Profane: Proceedings of a conference on archaeology, ritual and religion, Oxford, 1989*, Paul Garwood, ed., Oxford University Committee for Archaeology monograph 32 (1991), pp. 50–64.

Richard L. Burger's illustrated study *Chavín and the Origins of Andean Civilisation* (1992) presents the archaeological evidence for hallucinogens in Chavín and its surrounding cultures. I have added some speculations on their ritual uses in my article 'Enter the Jaguar: Psychedelic temple cults of ancient Peru', Strange Attractor Journal 2 (2005), pp. 17–34, also archived at http://mikejay.net/articles/.

Gerardo Reichel-Dolmatoff's research is recounted in *The Shaman and the Jaguar* (1975); he also published extensively on the ayahuasca art and cosmology of other Tukanoan groups in such books as *Shamanism and Art of the Eastern Tukanoan Indians* (1987) and *Beyond the Milky Way: Hallucinatory images of the Tukano Indians* (1978), both heavily illustrated.

The meaning of animal–human transformations in Amazon cultures is brilliantly discussed by Eduardo Viveiros de Castro in his article 'Cosmological Deixis and Amerindian Perspectivism', *Journal of the Royal Anthropological Institute* 4/3 (1998a), pp. 469–88, and his book *From the Enemy's Point of View: Humanity and divinity in an Amazonian society* (1992).

Drugs and Culture

Howard S. Becker's paper 'Becoming a Marihuana User' first appeared in the *American Journal of Sociology* 59 (November 1953), pp. 235–42. For more on the social history of drugs in 1950s America, see Jill Jonnes, *Hep-Cats, Narcs and Pipe Dreams* (1996).

The Culture of Kava

Vincent Lebot, Mark Merlin and Lamont Lindstrom's *Kava: The Pacific elixir* (1992) is an excellent single-volume account of the botany, history, ethnography and economics of kava. Changes in its cultural sanction and use are examined by Ron Brunton in *The Abandoned Narcotic: Kava and Cultural Instability in Melanesia* (1980). The first Western examination of its use was by the German pharmacologist Louis Lewin in his classic drug study

Phantastica: Die betaubenden und erregenden Genussmittel (1924), tr. as *Phantastica: Narcotic and stimulating drugs* (1931).

The Culture of Betel

The anthropology of consumption and luxury is explored in such influential works as Mary Douglas and Baron Isherwood's *The World of Goods: Towards an anthropology of consumption* (1979); Jack Goody's *Cooking, Cuisine and Class* (1982) and Pierre Bordieu's *Distinction: A social critique of the judgement of taste* (1984). Compared to food, however, the consumption of drugs has been relatively little studied from an anthropological perspective; a notable exception is the essay collection *Consuming Habits: Global and historical perspectives on how cultures define drugs*, Jordan Goodman, Paul Lovejoy and Andrew Sherratt, eds (1995; second edition 2007). It includes Stephen Hugh-Jones's paper 'Coca, Beers, Cigars and Yagé: Meals and anti-meals in an Amerindian community', pp. 46–64, which considers the roles of food and drugs in defining male and female social domains, and Eric Hirsch's 'Betel-nut "Bisnis" and Cosmology: A view from Papua New Guinea', pp. 86–97.

Dawn F. Rooney's *Betel Chewing Traditions in South-East Asia* (1993) is an attractive illustrated survey of the history and material culture surrounding betel; see also the film *Betelnut 'Bisnis': A story from Papua New Guinea* (2004), produced by SBS Independent in Australia in association with the National Film Institute of Papua New Guinea.

Drug Prohibitions

On alcohol in Roman antiquity, see *In Vino Veritas*, Oswyn Murray and Manuela Tecusan, eds, (1995); on alcohol and Islam, see Andrew Sherratt, 'Alcohol and its Alternatives', in *Consuming Habits*, pp. 11–45; and Mohammed Ali Albar, *The Problem of Alcohol and its Solution in Islam* (1986).

On the cultural dynamics underlying the prohibition of drugs in the modern West, see Axel Klein, *Drugs and the World* (2008). For a polemical extension of Max Weber's ideas into modern attitudes to drugs, see Thomas Szasz, *Ceremonial Chemistry: The ritual persecution of drugs, addicts and pushers* (1974).

Drug Subcultures

On the eighteenth-century London coffee house, see Markman Ellis, *The Coffee-House: A cultural history* (2004); on the wider picture, see Woodruff Smith's article 'From Coffeehouse to Parlour: The consumption of coffee, tea and sugar in north-western Europe in the seventeenth and eighteenth centuries', in *Consuming Habits*, pp. 142–157; and Wolfgang Schivelbusch's *Das Paradies, der Geschmack und die Vernunft: eine*

Geschichte der Genussmittel (1980) tr. David Jacobsen as *Tastes of Paradise* (1992). On the peyote cult, see Weston La Barre, *The Peyote Cult* (1959) and Omer C. Stewart, *Peyote Religion: A history* (1987).

For a sociological survey of the ayahuasca churches of modern Brazil, see Andrew Dawson, *New Era: New Religions: Religious transformations in contemporary Brazil* (2007); for a positive first-person account, Alex Polari de Alvergo, *Forest of Visions: Ayahuasca, Amazonian spirituality and the Santo Daime* (1999); on Brazil's other main ayahuasca church, the União do Vegetal, see Anthony Richard Henman, *Ayahuasca Use in a Religious Context* (1985), archived at www.erowid.org.

The Cultures of Ecstasy

On the emergence of ecstasy, see Matthew Collin, *Altered State* (1997); on the effect of ecstasy on mainstream consumer culture, Jim Carey's article 'Recreational Drug Wars: Alcohol versus Ecstasy', in *Ecstasy Reconsidered*, Nicolas Saunders, ed. (1997), pp. 20–27.

Chapter 2: From Apothecary to Laboratory

What Is A Drug?

On the origin of 'drug' as a pejorative term see John Parascandola, 'The Drug Habit: The association of the word 'drug' with abuse in American history' in *Drugs and Narcotics in History*, Roy Porter and Mikuláš Teich, eds (1995), pp. 156–67.

Drugs in Antiquity

On the role of drugs in classical antiquity, see Vivian Nutton, *Ancient Medicine* (2001); on Dioscorides, John Riddle, *Dioscorides on Pharmacy and Medicine* (1985). The *Materia medica* is published in various modern scholarly editions; one of the most accessible is Robert T. Gunther, ed., *The Greek Herbal of Dioscorides* (1934).

Renaissance Herbals

The early modern herbal is the subject of Agnes Arber's *Herbals: Their Origin and Evolution 1470–1670* (1912) and Frank J. Anderson's *An Illustrated History of the Herbals* (1977).

Witches and Flying Ointments

Narcotic Plants of the Old World (1979), edited by Hedwig Schleiffer, is a useful compendium of early texts on nightshades and 'flying ointments'. Due to nightshades' toxic and amnesiac effects, first-person accounts of intoxication are rare; a memorable and detailed description of smoking henbane seeds appears in Gustav Schenk's The Book of Poisons (1956).

The theory that the image of the witch straddling her broomstick represents the labial application of flying ointments originated with Michael J. Harner's article 'The Role of Hallucinogenic Plants in European Witchcraft', reprinted in his 1973 anthology Hallucinogens and Shamanism, pp. 125–50; and possibly also with Michael Harrison's The Roots of Witchcraft (1973). For a broader view of witches, Sabbats and flying ointments in the mythologies of the witch craze, see Stuart Clark's magisterial Thinking with Demons: The idea of witchcraft in early modern Europe (1997) or Brian Levack's The Witch-hunt in Early Modern Europe (1987).

On Andrés de Laguna, see Theodore Rothman, 'De Laguna's Commentaries on Hallucinogenic Drugs in Dioscorides' Materia medica', Bulletin of the History of Medicine, 46 (1972), pp. 562–7; and H. Friedenwald, 'Andrés a Laguna: A pioneer in his views on witchcraft', Bulletin of the History of Medicine 7 (1939), pp. 1037–48.

The Invention of Laudanum

Philip Ball's recent biography, The Devil's Doctor (2006), is an excellent introduction to Paracelsus's career. On the controversy over his 'laudanum', see Henry E. Sigerist, 'Laudanum in the Works of Paracelsus', Bulletin of the History of Medicine 9 (1941), pp. 530–544.

On Thomas Sydenham, see J. F. Payne, Thomas Sydenham (1900); on Dover, see D. N. Phear, 'Thomas Dover 1662–1743: Physician, privateering captain and inventor of Dover's Powder', Journal of the History of Medicine and Allied Sciences 9 (1954), pp. 139–56. On the strength of early laudanum preparations, see J. Worth Estes, 'John Jones' Mysteries of Opium Revealed: Key to historical opiates', Journal of the History of Medicine and Allied Sciences 34 (1979), pp. 200–9.

Linnaeus and the Enlightenment

The most accessible recent biography of Linnaeus is Wilfrid Blunt's Linnaeus: The Compleat Naturalist (1971). Linnaeus's Inebriantia (1762) is reprinted and discussed by Bo Holmstedt and Richard Evans Schultes in 'Inebriantia: An early interdisciplinary consideration of intoxicants and their effects on man', Botanical Journal of the Linnaean Society 101/2 (October 1989), pp. 181–98. The work was translated by Henry H. Parker for his PhD thesis, Linnaeus on Intoxicants: Pharmacology, sobriety and latinity in 18th century Sweden, University of Illinois (1977), and published as 'Carl Linnaeus' history of drugs: Inebriantia, English translation and commentary', Svenska Linné-Sällskapets Årsskrift (Yearbook of the Swedish Linnaeus Society) (1992/93), pp. 109–131. Holmstedt and Schultes include biographical information on Linnaeus's student Olof Reinhold Alander, who submitted *Inebriantia* as his doctoral thesis; the division of labour between professor and pupil is unknown, but the information and opinions are assumed to be mostly those of Linnaeus himself.

Early intoxications with mushrooms are detailed in Andy Letcher's *Shroom: A cultural history of the magic mushroom* (2006), a thorough and stimulating *tour d'horizon*. I have outlined the Victorian understanding of magic mushrooms, and their relation to fairy mythology, in my book *Emperors of Dreams: Drugs in the nineteenth century* (2000) and in a subsequent article, 'Mushrooms in Wonderland', *Fortean Times* 180 (2004), pp. 40–44, also archived at http://mikejay.net/articles/.

The First Synthetic Drugs

Accounts of the Pneumatic Institution's nitrous oxide experiments were published by Thomas Beddoes as *Notice of Some Observations Made at the Medical Pneumatic Institution* (1799), and by Humphry Davy as *Researches Chemical and Philosophical, chiefly concerning nitrous oxide and its respiration* (1800). Beddoes, Davy and the Pneumatic Institution are the subject of my book *The Atmosphere of Heaven* (2009).

Sertürner's isolation of morphine is discussed by J. E. Lesch in his article 'Conceptual Change in an Empirical Science: The discovery of the first alkaloids', *Historical Studies in the Physical Sciences* 2 (1981), pp. 306–328; and by Ryan J. Huxtable and Stephan K. W. Schwartz, 'The Isolation of Morphine: First principles in science and ethics', *Molecular Interventions* 1 (2001), pp. 189–91.

Opium and the Romantics

For Coleridge and opium, see Molly Lefebure, *Samuel Taylor Coleridge: A bondage of opium* (1977); Alethea Hayter, *Opium and the Romantic Imagination* (1968) and Richard Holmes, *Coleridge: Darker reflections* (1998), as well as Thomas De Quincey's essays *Samuel Taylor Coleridge* (1834–35) and *Coleridge and Opium-Eating* (1844).

De Quincey's *Confessions of an English Opium Eater* (1822) remains in print; recent biographies of De Quincey include Grevel Lindop, *The Opium-Eater* (1981); and Robert Morrison, *The English Opium-Eater* (2009).

The Club des Haschischins

Jacques-Joseph Moreau de Tours's *Haschisch et l'aliénation mentale* (1845) was translated into English as *Hashish and Mental Illness*, Gordon J. Bennett, tr. (1973), with a helpful introduction by Bo Holmstedt.

Théophile Gautier's 'Le Club des Haschischins' appeared in *Revue des deux mondes* in 1846 and is available in English online at www.lycaeum.org. Charles Baudelaire's *Du Vin et du haschisch* was first published in 1851 and revised in 1858, when he added his summary translation of De Quincey's *Confessions of an English Opium Eater*; all were collected as *Les Paradises artificiels* in 1860 and translated into English as *Artificial Paradises*, Stacy Diamond, tr. (1996). The Parisian hashish demimonde and its literary productions are discussed by Jerrold Siegel in *Bohemian Paris* (1986) and Emanuel Mickel in *The Artificial Paradises in French Literature* (1969).

Freud and Cocaine

Early texts on coca and cocaine are exerpted and collected in *The Coca Leaf and Cocaine Papers* (1975), edited by George Andrews and David Solomon. Sigmund Freud's 'Über Coca' is translated with additional correspondence and scientific material in Robert Byck, ed. and tr., *Cocaine Papers: Sigmund Freud* (1974).

The pharmaceutical 'cocaine boom' is analysed in H. Richard Friman's article 'Germany and the Transformation of Cocaine 1880–1920', in *Cocaine: Global Histories*, Paul Gootenberg, ed. (1999). Sherlock Holmes's cocaine use is most fully described by Arthur Conan Doyle in *The Sign of Four* (1890), and is discussed in my article 'Watson, the Needle!', *Darklore* 3 (2009), pp. 121–31, also archived at http://mikejay.net /articles/.

Addiction and Drug Control

On pharmaceutical drugs and hypodermic injection in the late nineteenth century, see Virginia Berridge and Griffith Edwards, *Opium and the People* (1981); Terry Parssinen, *Secret Passions, Secret Remedies* (1983); Marek Kohn, *Narcomania* (1987); Richard Davenport-Hines, *The Pursuit of Oblivion* (2001); and my *Emperors of Dreams* (2000).

On the birth of the criminal drug underground in America, see David Courtwright's *Dark Paradise* (2001); in Britain, Marek Kohn's *Dope Girls* (1992). On the emergence of the modern notion of 'drugs' and addiction, see Caroline Jean Acker, 'From All-Purpose Anodyne to Marker of Deviance: Physicians' attitudes to opiates in the US from 1890–1940', and John Parascandola, 'The Drug Habit', both in the collection *Drugs and Narcotics in History*, pp. 114–32 and 156–67, respectively; and Acker's subsequent book, *Creating the American Junkie* (2002). For an alternative view from the perspective of a drug user, see *Underworld of the East* (1935), the memoirs of James S. Lee, who offers a frank description of his recreational use of opium, cannabis, morphine, cocaine and other drugs in London, continental Europe and particularly the Far East between 1895 and 1914.

On the Harrison Act and the beginnings of drug control, see David F. Musto, *The American Disease* (1973) and his edited volume *Drugs in America: A*

Documentary History (2002). On the discovery of amphetamines and their subsequent medical and recreational careers, see Nicolas Rasmussen, *On Speed: The many lives of amphetamines* (2008). William Sargant's story is in his memoirs, *The Unquiet Mind* (1967).

Mescaline, LSD and Beyond

James Mooney's account of his peyote experience, 'The Mescal Plant and Ceremony', was published in *Therapeutic Gazette*, 12 [11] (1896), pp. 7–11; Silas Weir Mitchell's 'Remarks on the Effects of the *Anhalonium lewinii* (mescal button)' appeared in the *British Medical Journal* 2 (1896), pp. 1625–29. Havelock Ellis's reportage, 'A New Artificial Paradise', appeared in the *Contemporary Review* of January 1898. All are discussed in my *Emperors of Dreams* (2000). Extracts from mescaline texts by Henri Michaux, Stanisław Witkiewicz and others are included in my anthology *Artificial Paradises* (1999). See also Heinrich Klüver's *Mescal and Mechanisms of Hallucination* (1928). The protocols of Walter Benjamin's mescaline experiment of 1934 are included in *On Hashish*, Howard Eiland, ed. (2006), the most complete collection in English of Benjamin's drug texts.

The story of the discovery of LSD is told by Albert Hofmann in his *LSD: My problem child* (1979). The subsequent history of the drug is recounted by Jay Stevens in *Storming Heaven: LSD and the American dream* (1987). For the history of the Native American Church, see Omer Stewart, *Peyote Religion* (1987).

Alexander and Ann Shulgin tell their stories, along with reflections on their work and chemical syntheses of their discoveries, in *PIHKAL* (1991) and *TIHKAL* (1997). Other relevant and useful material is available at www.erowid.org

Drugs of the Future

Drugs of the future were the subject of much excited media reportage around the turn of the millennium, prompting speculations and prediction from commentators such as Francis Fukuyama in *Our Posthuman Future* (2002) and Susan Greenfield in *Tomorrow's People* (2003). Maartje Schermer, et al., 'The Future of Psychopharmacological Enhancements: Expectations and policies', *Neuroethics* 2 (2009), pp. 75–87 is perhaps a more realistic assessment of future trends.

Chapter 3: The Drugs Trade

Drugs of the New World

Jordan Goodman, ed., *Tobacco in History and Culture: An encyclopaedia*

(2005), is an invaluable reference for information regarding tobacco in both the Americas and Europe; see also Joseph Winter, ed., *Tobacco Use by Native North Americans* (2000). Hedwig Schleiffer, ed., *Sacred Narcotic Plant of the New World Indians* (1973), is a useful selection of texts that includes early Spanish accounts of peyote, mushrooms, ololiuqui and others. Spanish attitudes to New World hallucinogens are explored in the first volume of Antonio Escohotado's *Historia de las drogas* (1989), translated as *A Brief History of Drugs*, Kenneth A. Symington, tr., (1996); and in Fernando Cervantes' *The Devil in the New World: The impact of diabolism in New Spain* (1994).

Nicolás Monardes is situated in the context of the Age of Discovery in C. R. Boxer, *Two Pioneers of Tropical Medicine: Garcia d'Orta and Nicolás Monardes* (1963). For the history of tobacco in the Netherlands, see Georg A. Brongers, *Nicotiana Tabacum: The history of tobacco and tobacco smoking in the Netherlands* (1964). V. G. Kiernan's *Tobacco: A history* (1991) is a rich source of facts and anecdotes, from the European discovery of tobacco to the present. The illustrated anthology *Smoke: A global history of smoking* (2004), edited by Sander Gilman and Zhou Xun, illuminates the cultural diversity of the smoking complex.

The Psychoactive Revolution

On the medieval obsession with spices, see *Tastes of Paradise* and Jack Turner, *Spice* (2004). On their replacements, see Jordan Goodman, 'Excitantia: Or how Enlightenment Europe took to soft drugs', in *Consuming Habits*, pp. 121–41; and Rudi Mathee, 'Exotic Substances: The introduction and global spread of tobacco, coffee, tea and distilled liquor, 16th to 18th centuries', in *Drugs and Narcotics in History*, pp. 24–51.

The term 'psychoactive revolution' was coined by David Courtwright in *Forces of Habit: Drugs and the making of the modern world* (2001). The classic study of the role of sugar in history is Sidney Mintz's *Sweetness and Power* (1985). The effect of alcohol on Native Americans is explored by Peter C. Mancall in *Deadly Medicine: Indians and alcohol in early America* (1995).

Tobacco in China, Tea in Europe

For the extension of the European trade into China, see Timothy Brook, *Vermeer's Hat* (2008) and Frank Dikötter, Lars Laaman and Zhou Xun, *Narcotic Culture: A history of drugs in China* (2004).

The spread of tea into Europe is described by Roy Moxham in *Tea: Addiction, exploitation and empire* (2003) and by Alan and Iris Macfarlane in *Green Gold: The empire of tea* (2003). In his *Tastes of Paradise*, Wolfgang Schivelbusch considers why English taste in particular shifted from coffee to tea.

The Opium Wars

British opium policy in Bengal is analysed by David Edward Owen in *British Opium Policy in China and India* (1968); its wider outcomes are considered by Carl A. Trocki in *Opium, Empire and the Global Political Economy* (1999).

The narrative history of the Opium Wars has been told many times. *Foreign Mud* (1946) by Maurice Collis is a classic account, as is Jack Beeching's *The Chinese Opium Wars* (1975); the story is also well told, and set in a wider context, in Christopher Hibbert's *The Dragon Wakes: China and the West 1793–1911* (1970). The Chinese perspective, in which the remarkable character of Commissioner Lin is more fully explored, is presented by Hsin-Pao Chang in *Commissioner Lin and the Opium War* (1970) and by Arthur Waley in *The Opium War Through Chinese Eyes* (1958).

The Anti-Opium Campaign

Opium culture in nineteenth-century China is described by Keith McMahon in *The Fall of the God of Money* (2002), and sumptuously illustrated in K. Flow's *The Chinese Encounter with Opium* (2009). Peter Lee's *The Big Smoke: The Chinese art and craft of opium* (1999) is a hands-on guide to the techniques and utensils used in opium smoking. The picture of opium use in China has been substantially revised by Richard Newman's article 'Opium Smoking in Late Imperial China: A reconsideration', *Modern Asian Studies* 29/4 (1995), pp. 765–94; and particularly by Dikötter, Laaman and Zhou in *Narcotic Culture*. Previous histories such as Margaret Goldsmith's *The Trail of Opium: The Eleventh Plague* (1939) need to be read in the light of their findings.

For the anti-opium movement in Britain, see *Friend of China*, the journal of the Society for the Suppression of the Opium Trade, published from 1875, and *Opium and the People* (1981) by Virginia Berridge and Griffith Edwards, which also surveys the medical use of opiates in Victorian Britain and contrasts myth and reality in the classic image of the opium den. For more on the 'yellow peril' and opium scares and propaganda, see Barry Milligan's *Pleasures and Pains: Opium and the Orient in 19th-century British culture* (1995).

The early prohibitions of opium are discussed in Diana L. Ahmad, *The Opium Debate and Chinese Exclusion Laws in the Nineteenth-Century American West* (2007); David Musto, *The American Disease* (1973) and Richard Davenport-Hines, *The Pursuit of Oblivion* (2001). The British Royal Commission is the subject of John F. Richards's 'Opium and the British Empire: The Royal Commission of 1895', *Modern Asian Studies* 36 (2002), pp. 375–420. There is much new information on the consequences of opium prohibition in China in Dikötter, Laaman and Zhou's *Narcotic Culture*.

Temperance and Prohibition

On the emergence of the diagnosis of alcoholism, see Jean-Charles Sournia's *A History of Alcoholism* (1990). Histories of the Temperance movement tend to be national in scope. For Britain, see *Drink and the Victorians: The Temperance question in England 1815–72* by Brian Harrison (1994) and A. E. Dingle, *The Campaign for Prohibition in Victorian England* (1980), as well as Norman Kerr's *Journal of Inebriety* (1876–1914). On Germany, see James Roberts, *Drink, Temperance and the Working Classes in Germany* (1984); on America, see Ian Tyrrell, *Sobering Up: From Temperance to Prohibition in antebellum America 1800–1860* (1979), and Mark E. Lender, *Drinking in America: A history* (1982). On Prohibition in America, see John Kobler, *Ardent Spirits: The rise and fall of Prohibition* (1973) and Edward Behr, *Prohibition* (1997).

The 'War on Drugs'

The late twentieth-century 'war on drugs' has generated a vast contemporary literature, particularly of polemics against it; among the most lively are Dan Baum's *Smoke and Mirrors: The war on drugs and the politics of failure* (1996) and Mike Gray's *Drug Crazy* (1998). Axel Klein's *Drugs and the World* (2008) offers a global perspective on the effects of international drug control. Tom Feiling's *The Candy Machine: How cocaine took over the world* (2009) paints a vivid portrait of the effects of the trade on producer and transit countries. The case for maintaining the current international regime is made on the website of the body responsible for it, the United Nations Office on Drugs and Crime (www.unodc.org), where the counterproductive effects of its efforts are also acknowledged. See also Antonio Maria Costa, *Making Drug Control 'Fit for Purpose': Building on the UNGASS decade* (2008). Alternatives to the current system are explored by Robert MacCoun and Peter Reuter in *Drug War Heresies: Learning from other vices, times and places* (2001); and by the Transform Drug Policy Foundation in *After the War on Drugs: Blueprint for a regulated market* (2009).

Epilogue: The Decline of Tobacco

The iconic presence of tobacco in twentieth-century culture is celebrated in Richard Klein's *Cigarettes are Sublime* (1994). The scientific and legal struggle between tobacco corporations and public-health interests is chronicled in Allen Brandt's *The Cigarette Century* (2007). The World Health Organization's statistics on the global health costs of smoking, and the text of its Framework Convention on Tobacco Control, are on its website, www.who.int/tobacco. The cultures of tobacco in modern China and Japan are explored in Gilman and Zhou's *Smoke*. The corporate and public-health policies of Japan Tobacco are displayed on its website, www.jti.com.

Acknowledgments

This book was set in motion by my curatorial involvement in the *High Society* exhibition at Wellcome Collection, London. My thanks to Ken Arnold and his team at the Wellcome, and particularly to Emily Sargent for early discussions about the scope of the subject and how to organize it; our conversations are reflected in the chapter titles here.

I'm also very grateful to the Wellcome Library, on whose unique resources I drew heavily for both text and pictures: particularly to Phoebe Harkins and Ross MacFarlane for their enthusiasm and support, to Rowan de Saulles for making rare books and plates available for reproduction, and to Anna Smith for providing materials from Wellcome Images. Further thanks are due to Bruce Alexander, Phil Baker, Bal Croce, Max Decharne, Ben Goldacre, Stephen Hugh-Jones, Mark Nesbitt, Michael Rauner and Steve Rolles for their help in locating and accessing visual materials; to Sharon Messenger and Caroline Overy for hunting down academic journals; to Axel Klein for his thoughts on the manuscript; to Anthony Henman, Danny Kushlick and Michael Neve for many valuable discussions and insights; and, as ever, to Louise Burton for making it all as easy as possible.

Special thanks to my literary agent, Hannah Westland at Rogers, Coleridge & White, and to everyone at Thames & Hudson for their great enthusiasm for this project and their achievement in realizing it to such an exceptional standard.

Mike Jay

Picture Credits

Index

aconite 59; *see also* nightshades
Acosta, José de 109–10
addiction 13–14, 79–82, 91–100, 125, 149–53, 156–58, 157, 158, 159, 170–72
Afghanistan 167
Ah Sing 153, 154
alchemy 62, 63
alcohol 9, 22, 31, 35–36, 49, 69, 81, 128, 128–29, 131, 158–60, 159, 160, 161–64, 162, 163; *see also* Temperance movement, alcohol prohibitions
Alcohol Bureau (USA) 164
alcohol prohibitions 34–36, 39, 162–64, 163, 166, 167
alcoholism 158, 159
Alexander, Bruce 13–14
Alexander the Great 145
alkaloids 10–11, 68, 78
Alles, Gordon 100
Allom, Thomas 150–51
Amanita muscaria, see mushrooms, hallucincogenic: fly agaric
Amazon 10, 15–20, 16, 17, 43, 45
amphetamines 9, 39, 46, 100–1, 101, 107, 164
anaesthesia 53, 63, 77
animal experiments 13–14, 63, 76, 104
animal intoxication 11–14, 25, 63
Anadenanthera 14–20, 15, 17; *see also* DMT

Anglo-Oriental Society for the Suppression of the Opium Trade 153
Anslinger, Harry 164
apothecaries 53–54, 54, 65
Arabia 28, 35–37, 60
areca nut, *see* betel
Argentina 14, 90
Aristotle 50
Aschenbrandt, Theodor 90
aspirin 39, 39, 98
Aubert-Roche, Louis 88
Australia 24, 47, 129, 167
ayahuasca 4, 16, 18, 19, 28, 42, 43, 43–44, 49, 68
Ayer's Cherry Pectoral 38
Aztecs 60, 108, 109–10, 110, 121

Balzac, Honoré de 88
Bangladesh 8, *see also* Bengal
barbiturates 39, 98, 100
Baudelaire, Charles 89, 89–90
Bayer 36, 39, 98, 100
Becker, Howard S. 20–22, 21
Beddoes, Thomas 72–73, 73, 76–77, 88
belladonna 11, 59; *see also* nightshades
Bengal 82, 129, 136, 141–44, 141, 142–43
benzedrine 101, 164; *see also* amphetamines
betel 9, 28–34, 29, 30, 31, 32–33, 46, 49, 68–69, 130
bhang, see cannabis
Black, Wes 105
Bolivia 15

botanical gardens 55, 110, 112, 114
Bowrey, Thomas 82
Boxer Rebellion 156–57
Brande, Everard 69–72, 70
Brazil 10, 43–44, 109, 167
Brent, Bishop Charles 156
British East India Company 137, 138–39, 141–44, 141, 142–43, 147
British National Antarctic Expedition 64
British Royal Commission on Opium (1895) 156
bromides 95
Brown, Donald E. 10
Burma 9, 33, 34
Burroughs Wellcome Company 64, 92
Bush, President George H. W. 106
Bwiti religion 9

caffeine 78, 157
Cambodia 34, 155
Canada 9, 13, 13, 109, 167
cannabis 8, 21, 22, 36, 46, 49, 55–59, 56–57, 92, 107, 107, 164, 167, 168–69; *bhang* 68, 82; *ganja* 8; hashish 68, 82, 83, 84–85, 84–85, 86–87, 88, 89, 88–90; hemp 56–7, 82, 165; skunk 167
capsaicin 10–11
Caribbean 109, 119, 121, 124–25, 125, 128
catnip (*Nepeta cataria*) 11
Charcot, Jean-Martin 87, 90
Chavín 15–16, 15

Chen Cong 136
Chile 15, 109
chilli pepper 10–11
chillums, *see* pipes
China 9, 28, 108, 130, 133,
    136–41, 136, 137, 138,
    139, 140, 144–51, 148, 149,
    150–51, 156–58, 157, 170
Chinatowns 95, 98, 152, 153,
    156
chloral hydrate 91
chlorodyne 95
chloroform 95
chocolate 60, 69, 78, 108, 114,
    121, 120–23; *see also*
    theobromine
cigarettes 119, 157, 170–73,
    171, 173; *see also* tobacco
cigars 49, 109, 113; *see also*
    tobacco
Circe's potion 68, 69
classical antiquity 35, 35, 51,
    52, 53, 55, 69
Club des Haschischins 88, 89,
    88–90, 94
Coca-Cola 49, 92, 93
cocaine 9, 13, 28, 36, 38, 49,
    78, 90–95, 97, 99, 167
coca leaf 49, 50, 60, 78, 90, 91,
    114
coca wine 38, 90, 93
cocoa, *see* chocolate
codeine 78
coffee 9, 12, 31, 36, 69, 108,
    120–23
coffee houses 39–42, 40–41,
    138
Coleridge, George 79
Coleridge, Samuel Taylor 76,
    79, 81
Colorado, University of (USA)
    168–69
Colombia 10, 16–20, 167

Columbus, Christopher 109,
    112, 124
Comanche people 102
Conan Doyle, Arthur 94, 153
Cook, Captain James 27, 26–7
Cortés, Hernán 110
crack (cocaine) 167
Crowley, Aleister 48
Cruikshank, George 159

Datura 11, 53; *see also*
    nightshades
Davy, Humphry 73, 74–75, 76,
    79, 88
De Quincey, Thomas 79, 80,
    81–82, 88, 89, 90
diacetylmorphine, *see* heroin
Dickens, Charles 153, 154
dimethyltryptamine, *see* DMT
Dioscorides, Pedanius 51, 52,
    53, 55, 59, 60, 70, 107
DMT 14–20, 15, 16, 17, 18, 19,
    43; *see also* Anadenanthera,
    ayahuasca, Virola
Doll, Richard 170
dopamine 13
Doré, Gustave 153, 154
Dover, Thomas 64
Dover's Powder 64, 64–65
Dow Chemical Company 104
Drug Enforcement Agency
    (USA) 104, 106
drug prohibitions 34–9; coffee
    122, 122–23, kava 24;
    international 98, 100, 104,
    148, 156, 164–67; opium
    133, 144, 156–58; tobacco
    119–20, 167; *see also* alcohol
    prohibitions
drug smuggling: alcohol
    163–64; international
    164–67; opium into China
    141, 144, 146; tea 138–39

Dumas, Alexandre 88–89
Dutch East India Company
    (Vereenigde Oost-Indische
    Compagnie or VOC)
    134–35, 137, 147

Ebers papyrus 50
ecstasy 9, 28, 44, 45–46, 47,
    104, 107, 167
Egypt 36, 50, 51, 83, 84, 88
Ellis, Havelock 103
ephedra 100
ether 60, 95
Ethiopia 12

Fagron Pharmaceuticals 107
Fiji 25, 27
Flaubert, Gustave 89
fly agaric (*Amanita muscaria*),
    see mushrooms,
    hallucinogenic
flying ointments 59–60, 61; *see
    also* nightshades
France 84–85, 87, 88, 88, 89,
    116, 121, 129, 155, 156, 162
Freud, Sigmund 87, 90, 90–92
Fuchs, Leonhard 55–58

Gabon 12
Galenic medicine 54, 114
ganja, *see* cannabis
Gautier, Théophile 88, 88, 89
gender roles, drug use and
    27–28
Germany 53, 54, 60, 65,
    77–78, 90–92, 99, 103, 104,
    120, 122–23, 124, 160
Gillray, James 74–75
Gladstone, William 152
Golden Triangle 167
Göttingen, University of
    (Germany) 90
Grasset, Eugène–Samuel 96

Great Britain 39, 63, 69–77,
94, 100, 116–17, 119, 129,
137–39, 141–53, 162

Harrison Narcotic Tax Act
(1914) 98
hashish, see cannabis
Hastings, Warren 141
Hawaii 26
Heffter, Arthur 103
hemlock 59; see also
nightshades
hemp; see cannabis
henbane 59, see also
nightshades
herbals 55, 55, 56–57, 58, 112,
114
heroin 39, 49, 98, 99, 157, 167
Hippocratic medicine 51, 53,
63, 72
hookahs, see pipes
Hofmann, Albert 103, 105
Hong Kong 146
Huichol people 9, 111
Huxley, Aldous 103
hypodermic needles 92,
94–95, 96–97, 157–58

iboga 9
Iceland 163
India 9, 12, 31, 31, 46, 51, 129,
129, 132, 136, 141, 145, 167;
see also Bengal
Indonesia 9, 28, 33, 34, 124,
130, 133, 134–35
injection, see hypodermic
needles
International Conference on
Opium (The Hague, 1911)
156
International Opium
Commission (Shanghai,
1909) 156

ipecacuana 64
Ireland 160, 160
Islam 34–36, 124
Italy 90, 98, 160

jaguar transformation
(shamanism) 15, 15, 19–20
Jamaica 124, 128
James I (England) 114
Japan 130, 130, 131, 132, 136,
170
Japan Tobacco Inc. 170
Jardine, Matheson & Company
144, 153
Jerez, Rodrigo de 112
Jesuits (Society of Jesus)
109–10, 133
Jordan 37

kava 10, 23–28, 23, 24, 26, 27,
46, 49
Kendal's Black Drop
(laudanum) 79, 79
Kerr, Norman 162
ketamine 167
Kew Gardens (Great Britain) 17
khat 9, 11, 36, 49
kola nut 36
Koller, Carl 92
Korea 9

Laguna, Andrés de 60
Laos 155, 173
Lapland 66
laudanum 63–4, 64, 79, 79–81
laughing gas, see nitrous oxide
Lavoisier, Antoine 72
Leipzig, University of
(Germany) 103
liberty cap (Psilocybe
semilanceata), see
mushrooms,
hallucinogenic

Lin Zexu 146
Linnaeus, Carl 66, 67, 68,
67–69, 82
LSD 46, 49, 103–4, 105, 109,
164, 167

Madagascar 28
madak 133
'magic' mushrooms, see
mushrooms,
hallucinogenic: liberty cap
Malaysia 34
mandrake (mandragora) 53,
58, 59, see also nightshades
Mantegazza, Paolo 90
Mariani, Angelo 93
marijuana, see cannabis
Maudsley Hospital (Great
Britain) 100
Mayans 113
MDMA, see ecstasy
Medea 69
Melanesia 25–26
mephedrone 167
Merck Pharmaceutical
Company 90, 92, 104
Mering, Joseph von 98
Merrick, Joseph ('Elephant
Man') 96
mescaline 101–3, 104
Mexico 9, 42, 109–10, 110, 111,
130, 164, 165
Mezzrow, Milton 'Mezz' 21
Michaux, Henri 103
Mitchell, Silas Weir 103
Moctezuma 121
Modafinil 107
Monardes, Nicolás Bautista
112–13, 114
Monet, Claude 103
Mooney, James 101, 102, 103
Moreau de Tours, Jacques-
Joseph 84–85, 88, 88–90

morning glory, *see* ololiuqui

Morocco 164

morphine 14, 49, 77, 91, 92, 95, 157, 167

morphinomania 94–5, *see also* narcomania

moxa 133, 157

Mughals 31

mushrooms, hallucinogenic 12, 22, 60, 69–72, 71, 109, 110, 164; fly agaric (*Amanita muscaria*) 12, 72; liberty cap (*Psilocybe semilanceata*) 60, 69–72, 71; *teonanácatl* (*Psilocybe aztecorum*) 109, 110

Myanmar, *see* Burma

Nadar (Félix Tournachon) 88

naloxone 14

Napoleon Bonaparte 84

narcomania 95, 96

Narcotics Bureau (USA) 164

Native Americans 14–20, 60, 101–3, 109–14, 119, 125, 128, 128–29, 153, 172; *see also* Amazon, Aztecs, Comanche, Huichol, Mayans, Sioux, Taíno, Tukano

Native American Church 41–42, 104

Neander, Johann 116

needles, *see* hypodermic needles

de Nerval, Gérard (Gérard Labrunie) 88

Netherlands 107, 112, 116, 118, 120, 130, 133, 134–35, 137, 141, 147, 156, 162

neurasthenia 95, 158

neurochemistry 13, 14, 106–7

New Guinea 9, 28, 124

nicotine 78, 171–72

Niemann, Alfred 90

nightshades 11, 53, 59–60, 61

nitrous oxide 49, 72–77, 74–75, 77, 79, 88

Nixon, President Richard 167

Norway 163

ololiuqui 109, 110

opiates, *see* codeine, heroin, laudanum, opium, morphine

opium 39, 53, 58, 59, 63–64, 67, 79, 80, 79–82, 91, 92, 145, 163, 167; in British India (Bengal) 141–44, 141, 142–146; in China 133, 134, 134, 144–51, 148, 149, 150–51, 167, 170; *see also* laudanum

opium dens 98, 148–49, 153, 154–55, 158

Opium Wars 146, 147, 148, 151

Ostade, Adriaen van 116

Owsley, *see* Augustus Owsley Stanley III

Pacific region 10, 23–28, 46, 129

Padua, University of (Italy) 55

Palmerston, Lord (Henry John Temple) 151

Paracelsus (Theophrastus von Hohenheim) 62, 63, 73

Parke-Davis Pharmaceutical Company 92, 96, 103

Pershing, General John J. 170

Persia 141, 156

Peru 15, 15, 63, 90

Peter the Great 120

peyote 9, 42–3, 101, 102, 103, 104, 110, 111; *see also* mescaline, Native American Church

piracetam 107

Piper methysticum, *see* kava

pipes: DMT 14; hookahs 36, 37, 87 129; opium 80, 133, 136, 136, 148–50, 148, 149, 150–51, 153, 154–55, 157; tobacco 2–3, 36, 37, 113, 116–17, 119

Philippines 29, 130, 156

plant drugs, evolution of 10–11, 13

Pneumatic Institution 72–73, 76

Poland 72

Portugal 129, 130, 132, 133, 136, 141, 144, 147, 156

Pope Julius III 60

Previati, Gaetano 84–85

Priestley, Joseph 72

Prohibition, *see* alcohol prohibition, Volstead Act

Prozac 107

Psilocybe spp., *see* mushrooms, hallucinogenic

psilocybin 72

psychopharmacology 49, 53, 68, 104–7

Quakers (Society of Friends) 153

Rat Park experiments 13–14

Reichel-Dolmatoff, Gerardo 16–20

Reynolds, John Russell 92

Ricci, Matteo 133

Ritalin 107

Rohmer, Sax 156

Royal Institution (Great Britain) 74–75

Russia 71, 120

Salvia divinorum 167

Sami people 66

Sandoz Laboratories 103–4
San Francisco Opium
    Exclusion Act (1875) 156
Santo Daime 42, 43, 43–44
Santo Domingo (Haiti) 124
Sargant, William 100
Schultes, Richard Evans 16
self-experimentation 72–92,
    100–1, 104, 165
serotonin 13
Serra, Raimundo Irineu 43, 43
Sertürner, Friedrich 77–78, 78
Shakespeare, William 59
Shaftesbury, seventh Earl
    (Anthony Ashley-Cooper)
    153
shamanism 10, 15–20, 45, 59,
    72, 109–11
shisha pipes, see pipes: hookah
Shulgin, Alexander 104, 106,
    106
Sime, Sydney 86
sinicuichi 110
Sioux people 101
skunk, see cannabis
'smart drugs' 107
Smithsonian Institution (USA)
    101
snuff, DMT 15–19, 15, 16, 17;
    tobacco 119, 123, 133
Society for the Study of
    Inebriety (Great Britain) 162
Solomon Islands 30
solvents 10, 49
Somalia 49
Southey, Robert 76
Sowerby, James 71, 72
Spain 46, 112, 114, 119, 130,
    167
Spanish Inquisition 112
Spallanzani, Lazzaro 79
spices 51, 64, 122–23
Spruce, Richard 17

Stanley, Augustus Owsley III,
    106
Sudan 36
sugar 9, 14, 124–28, 125, 127,
    167
sulphonal 95
Sweden 67–69, 129, 163
Switzerland 55, 63, 103, 164
Sydenham, Thomas 63,
    63–64, 64, 79, 82
Syrian rue (*Peganum harmala*)
    68

Taíno people 109, 112
Taiwan 32, 137
tea 9, 36, 49, 69, 108, 120–23,
    124, 136–39, 137, 138, 139,
    140
Temperance movement
    158–60, 159, 160, 161, 171
Teniers, David (the younger)
    12
teonanácatl (*Psilocybe aztecorum*),
    see mushrooms,
    hallucinogenic
Thailand 9, 34, 46, 167
theobromine 78, 121
Theophrastus 50
thornapple, see *Datura*
tobacco 2–3, 11, 12, 22, 28, 36,
    36, 37, 49, 69, 109–20, 110,
    115, 126, 129–33, 139, 167,
    170–73, 171, 173; see also
    cigarettes, cigars, drug
    prohibitions, pipes, snuff
Tonga 25, 26
Treaty of Nanking (1842) 146
Treves, Sir Frederick 96
Tukano people 16–20
Turkey 51, 52, 68, 167

United Nations Office on
    Drugs and Crime 167

United Nations Single
    Convention on Narcotic
    Drugs (1961) 164
United States 9, 20–22, 45, 80,
    95, 98, 101, 102, 103–7, 152,
    156, 158, 160, 163–67, 163,
    165, 166, 168–69, 172
Uppsala, University of
    (Sweden) 67

Vanuatu 27
Veronal 98, 100; see also
    barbiturates
Victoria, Queen (Great
    Britain) 92, 146
Vietnam 155
Virola spp. 16–20, 16
Volstead Act (1919) 163

'war on drugs' 167
Webber, John 26
Weber, Max 39
West Africa 9, 12, 130, 132, 167
Wilde, Oscar 153
witch craze 59–60, 61, 109–10
Witkiewicz, Stanisław 103
wolfsbane 59; see also
    nightshades
Wordsworth, William 79, 103
World Health Organization 8,
    172, 173

Xochipilli 111

ya'aba 9; see also
    amphetamines
Yellow Peril 152, 156
Yemen 9, 11
Yongzheng edict (1729) 133